Jake J

What They're Saying
Good News f

D0355173

"Those of us in the media are often g_____ _____ ____ _____ ___ ____ than good news. That's why Mort Crim is so refreshing. He calls each of us to be a spiritual Columbus and look at the world differently from the hard-nosed realists around us and in the media. Thanks Mort, for charting a new course and giving us some *Good News for a Change!*"

KERBY ANDERSON
PRESIDENT OF PROBE MINISTRIES, GUEST HOST OF "POINT OF VIEW" (USA RADIO NETWORK) AND "OPEN LINE" (MOODY BROADCASTING NETWORK)

"The felicitous title of this book is enough to attract readers weary of bad news in these last days of the Twentieth Century. But it's what is inside the cover that will lift the human spirit and renew faith in God and humanity, as Mort Crim present gems of thought in his most engaging anecdotal style. He shares the really good news of the Gospel message as expressed in down-to-earth living experiences. A helpful and rewarding book"

D. JAMES KENNEDY, PH.D.
SENIOR MINISTER, CORAL RIDGE PRESBYTERIAN CHURCH

"I have had the opportunity to read many of these insightful meditations written by my friend, Mort Crim. These 'second thoughts' are quite often biblically inspired and reflect on the 'nitty gritty' of daily living from a faith perspective. In that sense, they are almost like little homilies! Truly this book is full of 'good news!' Happy reading."

ADAM CARDINAL MAIDA
ARCHBISHOP OF DETROIT

"Mort Crim's fine book provides not only inspiration, but common sense. It also provokes an almost irresistible urge to underline key passages for emphasis—and long-term access"

MICHAEL MEDVED
TALK SHOW HOST ON THE SALEM RADIO NETWORK, FILM CRITIC AND AUTHOR

"Not many journalists are willing to reveal and share their faith as boldly as Mort Crim. *Good News for a Change!* says the things many of us wish we had the courage to say."

DOUG POLING
FORMER CBS NEWS CORRESPONDENT

Good News
for a Change!

Mort Crim

foreword by Bill and Gloria Gaither

VINE
BOOKS

SERVANT PUBLICATIONS
ANN ARBOR, MICHIGAN

Vine Books is an imprint of Servant Publications especially designed to serve evangelical Christians.

Published by Servant Publications
P.O. Box 8617
Ann Arbor, Michigan 48107

Cover photograph: CORBIS/Kevin R. Morris
Author photograph: Bob Foran, Ann Arbor, Michigan

99 00 01 10 9 8 7 6 5 4 3 2

Printed in the United States of America
ISBN 1-56955-182-0

LIBRARY OF CONGRESS CATALOGING-IN-PUBLICATION DATA

Crim, Mort.
    Good news for a change! / Mort Crim ; foreword by Bill and Gloria Gaither.
        p.   cm.
    ISBN 1-56955-182-0 (alk. paper)
    1. Christian life.   I. Title.
BV4510.2.C69   1999
242—dc21   99-32752
                                            CIP

Dedication

I dedicate this book
with much love
to my sister, Barbara,
and to her children,
Anne, Bryan, and Naomi

Acknowledgments

Everyone whose life has touched mine has contributed in some way to this book.

I'm especially grateful to my parents, Albert and Ocie Crim, for *doing it right*, and to my grandparents, Alvah Morton and Mary Francis Crim. My family is in large measure responsible for any successes I have enjoyed either personally or professionally. They are not, however, to blame for my mistakes—most of which I've managed to make without assistance.

A special thanks to Servant Publications and to Bert Ghezzi, my friend and editor, who suggested this book and helped pull it together.

Preface

News has the power to change us.

Bad news can leave us depressed. Too much can make us cynical.

Good news can inspire us. Energize us. Infuse us with hope.

We know this is true in our personal lives. We are instantly—sometimes permanently—changed by bad news:

- A letter stating that someone we love is seriously ill …

- A termination notice from our employer …

- A phone call that our teenager has been in an accident …

But *good* news also has the power to change:

- A job promotion for one of our children …

- The birth of a child—or grandchild …

- A good medical report from the lab …

Not only does news change our mood, it also changes our bodies. Numerous tests have proven conclusively that what's going on in our minds and emotions triggers changes in our body chemistry. The old lines "This job is killing me" and "I'm dying to get out of this relationship" turn out to be more than just rhetoric.

It was because I believed *news matters* that I decided early in life to become a journalist. Just as personal news changes us individually, the news we receive collectively changes us as a nation.

All of us can remember headlines that impacted us so forcefully that our lives, literally, were never the same again:

- President Kennedy Assassinated …
- Man Lands on the Moon …
- President Nixon Resigns …
- Space Shuttle *Challenger* Explodes …
- Berlin Wall Falls …
- President Clinton Impeached …

These and hundreds of other stories have changed us. They have changed our perception of the world, and changed how we feel about our nation and about our own lives. Unfortunately, stories of tragedy and human failing now fill most of our news space. And with the proliferation of cable TV and Internet news sources, what used to be a trickle of information has now become a flood.

There have been consequences to this colossal increase in the dissemination of bad news. It is no coincidence that we have seen, simultaneously, an increased cynicism about our society—especially about our political system and our leaders.

While I chose news reporting as a career, my father spent his life as a clergyman. I used to joke with him that his job was to tell the *Good News* so that people could handle the *bad news* they got from me.

Today, it's no joke. The *Good News* Dad delivered—that life has meaning, that we were created for a purpose, that we are all members of one family, and that God loves us—is absolutely essential if we're to find our way in a world that seems increasingly to have lost its sense of direction.

While all news has the power to change us, none has the power to change our lives as meaningfully and as permanently as does that *Good News* to which my father and mother were committed. I have personally seen broken lives mended, shattered relationships rebuilt, and hopelessness replaced by inexplicable enthusiasm through the power of the *Good News*.

What is this *Good News*? It's a message so profoundly simple it can be summarized in the words of a song written by my good friend Bill Gaither: *Loving God and Loving Each Other*. Dad knew that the *Good News* isn't complicated. He understood faith at its essence. It's so simple, in fact, that even the least sophisticated shepherd two thousand years ago could grasp it. At the core, what we find is really *good news for a change!*

I hope the following pages will provide some perspective on your world, renew your hope for the future, and help balance the largely negative view provided by the mass media. Perhaps they will even change *you*.

Foreword

We've known Mort Crim since our college days at Anderson University and have always applauded his candor and been intrigued by his ability to stand apart from the crowd and view life through a different window.

Years of experience in the field of journalism have only sharpened that insight. His unique perception constantly focuses on the core of Christ's gospel rather than on human trimmings.

"What would Jesus do?" is not a new concept for Mort. He's been asking that question for a long time and, in some instances, with some resistance from the church.

What we've always admired about Mort is his willingness to take risks. During his years as a news broadcaster, Mort lived out Christ's mandate to be "salt and light" in the real world.

Now that he has left the television anchor desk, it is delightful and refreshing to see Mort spending much of his time and energy communicating truths that transcend the four walls of the traditional church.

At this stage of our lives, we enjoy being around people who help put things into perspective. Because of his world-view, diverse travels, and years of newscasting and reporting,

Mort has developed a very healthy and balanced perspective on life—which still reflects his distinctively Christian vision.

Good News for a Change! presents a glimpse of life through a *different window* from a friend who knows the power of good news in the lives of people today.

Bill and Gloria Gaither

Good News

> I have come that they may have life, and
> have it to the full.
>
> JOHN 10:10, NIV

Nearly two thousand years ago a young radical stepped into history with a message so vital that it has been known ever since simply as "the Good News." This young visionary was a genius at seeing the potential in a man or woman or situation. He never overlooked what was. Yet he always looked beyond to what could be.

To those who mourned the future of humanity, he said, "Because I live, you also will live." He taught that in the ultimate economy of existence, good finally will overcome evil. Life will overcome death. Light will dispel darkness. He taught that people and societies can be changed. He taught that every person has intrinsic value, that every individual has ultimate worth.

To those who found life totally frustrating or unbearably

boring, he announced that life could be meaningful and vibrant. To those drifting aimlessly in a sea of intellectual confusion, he proclaimed that life could be purposeful. To the sick, he offered health. To the slave, he promised freedom.

It was more than what he said that attracted people to his way. It was also who he was, what he did, how he lived, how he loved, how he died, and how he conquered death.

Jesus not only told it like it was, he showed how it ought to be. Everyone who would follow him must do likewise.

> *Christ appears the one reasonable, natural, certain thing in all the universe. In him all broken lines unite. In him all scattered sounds are gathered in harmony.*
>
> PHILLIPS BROOKS
>
> ～
>
> *When Jesus Christ utters a word, he opens his mouth so wide that it embraces all heaven and earth, even though the word be but a whisper.*
>
> MARTIN LUTHER

Serving in the World

> Let your light so shine before men, that they
> may see your good works and give glory to
> your Father who is in heaven.
>
> MATTHEW 5:16, RSV

*J*ournalism was not my first career choice.

Like most young people, I struggled with the decision: What should I do with my life?

As the son of a clergyman, I recognized the Christian ministry as one valid pathway to service. From my teenage years through my early twenties I gave serious thought to making *that* my life's work. Specifically, I entertained the notion of becoming an Air Force chaplain, where I could both minister and be around airplanes (for a fledgling pilot, the best of all possible worlds, perhaps).

Many members of my family were in religious vocations—pastors, teachers, missionaries. However, my grandfather was a judge, his father had been in the Indiana state legislature, and two of my aunts were in show business. My growing-up years were thus influenced by politics and the entertainment industry as well as by the church.

I was nearly thirty before deciding that my *calling* was journalism—specifically broadcast journalism. I suppose reporting and presenting news on television and radio combines some facets of show business, politics, and teaching.

Central to my decision was a deep desire to serve. To enlighten. To open minds. To make the world a better place.

I believed then—and I believe now—that ministry is not the exclusive work of ordained clergy. To the contrary, if the Scriptures are clear on anything, they are crystal-clear on this: every disciple of Christ is called to serve. Each has different gifts, different aptitudes, different talents, and different interests. Yet all are called to comfort, to heal, to help, to proclaim God's love, and to encourage.

I used to think of the word *minister* as a noun. Sometimes it is. Over my lifetime, however, I've learned that it's also a verb! We don't have to *be* it in order to do it.

> Take that gift that God has entrusted to you, no matter how humble it may seem to be, and use it in the service of Christ and your fellow human beings. He will make it glow and shine like the very stars of heaven.
>
> JOHN SUTHERLAND BONNELL

Not Your Eleven O'Clock News

> *It is better to light one candle than to curse the darkness.*
>
> AMERICAN PROVERB

*I*f the news makes you feel bad, here's some unreported information that may improve your mood.

Have you heard about the church that helped Clare get off drugs and welfare, and start a successful business? Churches tend to make news only when their ministers or their finances are in trouble.

Have you heard about Conni, a student at Howard University in Washington, D.C.? She takes city kids from poor neighborhoods, puts them on a patch of land, and teaches them to farm. Students like Conni tend to make news only when they overdose on cocaine or get arrested for possession of a controlled substance.

Maybe you haven't heard about Scott in Berkeley, California. No wonder. He's not famous. He works at a deli where he takes leftover food to street people who have no homes and little hope. But if Scott had robbed that shop, a lot of people would know his name.

All across this nation, people are helping people. They are reaching out to abused children, battered spouses, teenage mothers, AIDS patients, and drug addicts.

These aren't the stories likely to make the eleven o'clock news. But they're real. As real as marriages that survive, friendships that last, teachers who teach, and workers who put in an honest day's work.

While tragic headlines charge the atmosphere with doom, countless constructive acts of kindness light up the dark corners of our world.

If we're cynical, it's because we've allowed the lightning to blind us to the candles.

> *Dear children, let us not love with words or tongue but with actions and in truth.*
>
> 1 JOHN 3:18, NIV

The Last Measure

> *Man shall not live by bread alone, but by every word that proceeds from the mouth of God.*
>
> MATTHEW 4:4, RSV

Some people hoard their assets until the very end. Then, in a final bid to purge their greed, they bequeath their possessions to some charity or public foundation. For other people, generosity is a way of life.

That's how it was with Charles of Seattle. Charles wasn't a wealthy man. He lived comfortably, selling groceries from his little corner store. But the way Charles ran his business, he never had a chance to get rich. For one thing, he gave too many groceries away to those who couldn't pay. He also sold a lot on credit. Charles had a very poor memory, too, especially if he knew his debtor was hard up and unable to pay.

So, knowing the kind of person Charles was in life, his customers and other friends weren't at all surprised to learn that Charles' last thought was for others. Just before he died, from bullet wounds inflicted by a young robber, Charles asked that the eight hundred dollars worth of canned goods on his shelves be given to Seattle's poor.

Charles was a grocer who did not live by bread alone.

Give in simplicity to all who need, not doubting to whom you shall give and to whom not. Give to all, for to all God wishes gifts to be made of his goodness.

SHEPHERD OF HERMAS

~

He who gives alms in secret is greater than Moses.

ANCIENT JEWISH SAYING

Called to Care

A perceptive observer once said that he thinks many essentially kind and decent people are simply suffering from "compassion fatigue."

Our capacity for sympathy can become exhausted by overuse. And yet, love and concern are so crucial to the Christian reality and so vital to salvaging wasted humanity that we must not become weary of doing good. Jesus was in the business of reclaiming people—saving lost lives. Of course he reclaimed individuals. He rescued at the personal level.

In our complex and populous society, however, Christ's disciples have a broader responsibility. We must remember that Jesus not only saved from the spiritual slavery of selfishness and meaninglessness, but he also fed the hungry and healed the sick. Our task as Christians, therefore, is not only to introduce purpose and meaning and the power to overcome in life. Our job includes feeding the hungry, sheltering the homeless, and caring for the ill. This is not a question of political philosophy. It is not a question of competing systems of government. For the Christian, it is a question of the gospel's mandate. What do we care about most? Programs? Property? Or people?

> *Compassion is the chief law of human existence.*
>
> FYODOR DOSTOYEVSKY

A Christian at Work

In our era, the road to holiness necessarily passes through the world of action.

DAG HAMMARSKJÖLD

Today no one lacks an opportunity who is willing to serve other people. In my vocation as a broadcaster and in countless other secular pursuits, the needs are painfully visible. Sometimes we laypeople can step through doors of opportunity rarely—if ever—opened to religious professionals. While we don't officiate at weddings, bury the dead, or break Communion bread, we are positioned to perform acts no less sacred—like injecting meaning into a life that has none or introducing God to a person who because of prejudice, pride, or guilt would never discuss such personal matters with a minister.

By vocation Jesus was trained as a carpenter. Most of his life was spent in a woodworking shop. Paul was a professional tentmaker. There no mention in the New Testament that he ever gave up that secular vocation. Presumably, what Paul did for a living supported his Christian service.

It is great when *doing* and *being* converge for a person, as they have for me. I find being a Christian and doing my job as a journalist not only compatible but significantly related. As a newsman, I have always lived and worked "where the action is." I have interviewed some of the most interesting, famous, and powerful people in the world. I have reported on events that nudged the course of history. Viewing events from a Christian perspective has helped me make sense of a world where so much *seems* senseless.

Blessed is he who has found his work. Let him ask no other blessedness. He has a work, a life purpose.

THOMAS CARLYLE

~

Where our work is, there let our joy be.

TERTULLIAN

Point of View

Someone asked me the other day if a journalist could hold any specific religious beliefs and still be an objective reporter. Is it possible, he wondered, for a reporter to accept any personal philosophy or theology and still remain unbiased in viewing life and reporting on it?

Like so many questions, this one sounds reasonable until we look more closely at it. If commitment to certain ideals precludes a journalist from giving a fair shake to opposing concepts, then, perhaps, we must also conclude that a happily or unhappily married reporter could not impartially cover a divorce proceeding. Or that a female reporter could not report objectively on abortion. Or that a journalist with school-age children could not be fair in covering a school board meeting or school taxes.

We all wear many hats, play many roles, and function in many ways. Objectivity and fairness are not products of the roles we play. These qualities come from a state of mind and commitment. Indeed, an honest faith, born of love for truth, might well be a reporter's best hope for genuine objectivity.

Some may be colorblind but others see the bright hues of sunrise. Some may have no religious sense, but others live and move and have their being in the transcendent glory of God.

WILLIAM CECIL DAMPIER

A wise man's heart guides his mouth.

PROVERBS 16:23, NIV

Bad-News Bearers

> 'Tis incredible what a vast good a little truth might do.
>
> ALEXANDER POPE
>
> The truth will make you free.
>
> JOHN 8:32, RSV

On a flight from Cape Kennedy to New York one morning, I sat next to David Brinkley. Discussing our roles as newsmen, we agreed that most people are personally upset by bad news. They don't like it. Furthermore, we agreed that a lot of people resent those who have to present the unfortunate and unpleasant truth. It had been only a few weeks since the 1968 Democratic convention. David told me he had received thousands of letters protesting the way radio and television had covered the demonstrations in Chicago during that event. He was obviously disturbed by this massive, negative reaction. The famous Brinkley grin was gone as he said, "You know, Mort, I'm convinced people really don't want us to tell it like it is."

He was right. Too many people would rather remain serene in their illusions than be agitated by facts. This is why prophets and preachers in every age have been prime targets of anger, even violence. They may be most assailable when they are most faithful to the truth.

Candor is costly. Yet self-deceit costs even more. It can be a lethal mistake to demand that our messengers, either journalists or clergy, entertain us rather than inform us.

> *He who does not bellow the truth, when he knows the truth, makes himself the accomplice of liars and forgers.*
>
> CHARLES PÉGUY

"Puppy" Love

> *Fear always springs from ignorance.*
>
> RALPH WALDO EMERSON
>
> ~
>
> *Love ... always protects, always trusts,*
> *always hopes, always perseveres.*
>
> 1 CORINTHIANS 13:6-7, NIV

*T*hey called their Italian grandfather "Puppy." And he *was* as Italian as he was proud of the heritage. He had immigrated to America with his beloved wife, Clementina. Their names are on a plaque at Ellis Island. But Clementina never knew that. She died before the plaque was put up, and Puppy never got over losing her. For twenty-eight years, he remained a widower, living with his children and five grandchildren.

The grandkids loved Puppy, but one of his behaviors made them a bit apprehensive. He had this eccentric—even weird—habit of sitting quietly in his favorite chair, writing mysteriously on index cards. The kids wondered, "Is Puppy spying on us? Will he report our misconduct to Mom and Dad?"

Until Puppy died, they worried a little and wondered a lot. Only after he was buried did they know. Inside dresser drawers in his room they found hundreds of those index cards, carefully held together by rubber bands. The cards meticulously documented not the transgressions of his anxious grandchildren, but the thousands of prayers he had said for them and for their parents.

We fear what we don't understand, and fear breeds mistrust. We build trust by learning more about what people do and why they do it.

> *The prayer of a righteous man is powerful and effective.*
>
> JAMES 5:16, NIV

Invisible Yet Real

> Science has not closed, and will never close,
> the soul's east window of surprise.
>
> RUFUS M. JONES
>
> ~
>
> With all your science, can you tell me how
> and from where it is that light comes into
> the soul?
>
> HENRY DAVID THOREAU

I concede the difficulty modern people encounter as they attempt to deal with the issue of faith. Many people, for example, limit reality to what they can perceive through the five senses. In accepting as real things that we touch, taste, smell, hear, and see, must we deny the existence of those realities that are beyond such perception?

Were X rays unreal—nonexistent—before we devised the means to discover them? Were distant stars, only recently detected by the Hubble telescope, not real until we knew they were there?

In a scientific age accustomed to seeing yesterday's heresies become today's dogmas, we might expect that dogmatic certainties denying God's existence would be considered unscientific since they can't be proven. The Christian does not wait for all the laboratory reports to come in before declaring faith. Like Thomas Jefferson, we hold some truths to be self-evident.

> *Faith is the assurance of things hoped for, the conviction of things not seen. For by it the men of old received divine approval.*
>
> HEBREWS 11:1-2, RSV

Cross Beams

> The cross is salvation. In the cross is life. In the cross is protection from enemies. In the cross is the infusion of heavenly sweetness.
>
> THOMAS À KEMPIS

*T*here was nothing special about the cross. Hundreds, probably thousands, of common criminals and traitors had suffered similar humiliating deaths on similar crosses.

But the Jewish prophet they nailed up that day was somebody special. His life had been special. His death was special. His special brand of love was to become the ultimate mind-expanding power.

That cross marked the spot where history was divided into B.C. and A.D. It continues to mark the intersection at which individual lives move toward meaning or into oblivion. To fully recognize that cross is to come to terms with death: Not just physical death, but death to selfishness, to fear, and to despair.

That symbol of death is equally the symbol of life. For

on that cross, death was conquered by love. It is a cross with two beams: one horizontal, as though embracing all mankind in shared suffering, the other vertical, as though pointing toward ultimate meaning. The vertical beam is anchored solidly in the here and now, but it directs our attention to the hereafter. Jesus' life and death give meaning to ours.

Those who belong to Christ Jesus have crucified the sinful nature with its passions and desires.

GALATIANS 5:24, NIV

The cross does not abolish suffering, but transforms it, sanctifies it, makes it fruitful, bearable, even joyful, and finally victorious.

JOSEPH RICKABY

A Love That Is Both/And

> Not to hurt our humble brothers and sisters
> is our first duty to them. But to stop there
> is a complete misapprehension of the inten-
> tions of Providence. We have a higher mis-
> sion. God wishes that we should succor
> them when they require it.
>
> FRANCIS OF ASSISI

When Jesus was asked which commandments he considered the most impor-
tant, he said, "The most important one is this: … 'Love the
Lord your God with all your heart, with all your soul, with
all your mind, and with all your strength.' The second
most important commandment is this: 'Love your neighbor as you love yourself.' There is no other commandment
more important than these two" (Mk 12:29-31, TEV).

Jesus was saying that it's just as important to love fellow
human beings as it is to love God. This gospel that
demands our love is especially dangerous when we begin to
apply it to specific areas of conflict and unrest in social life.

The continuing argument over whether Christians

should be concerned with saving souls or saving bodies has always seemed to me a senseless debate. The Christian gospel concerns itself with the wholeness of human beings. It speaks to all of our needs—spiritual, emotional, and physical. To be relevant in today's world, we must stop looking at people in an either/or fashion and see them as both/and. Like Jesus, we must see human beings as *both* spiritual *and* physical, and undertake to serve all their needs.

I think in terms not only of body-hunger, but of mind- and soul-hunger. The church must always go on her mission in the world with the Bible in her hand.

F. DONALD COGGAN

Suppose a brother or sister is without clothes and daily food. If one of you says to him, "Go, I wish you well; keep warm and well fed," but does nothing about his physical needs, what good is it?

JAMES 2:15-16, NIV

Better to Give

This only is charity, to do all, all that we can.

JOHN DONNE

*I*t's better to give than to receive. For most of us, that's a nice thought—a worthy sentiment, perhaps—but to Ed and Claire it was a proven principle. Each year for many years, the couple globe-trotted for a few weeks, sharing their skills and themselves with people less fortunate than they.

Both Ed and Claire were doctors. He was a surgeon and she a retired pediatrician. But periodically Ed left his practice in Northhampton, Massachusetts, and Claire came out of retirement and they took their much-needed medical knowledge and instruments to places such as Kenya, Nigeria, Guinea, or Vietnam. They doctored needy Navajos on Arizona reservations. During the Biafran war, they took care of thousands of starving children and built a hospital from scratch. Once Ed performed surgery under the glare of a detached car headlight hooked to a battery.

When they were in their mid-sixties, Ed and Claire did

this instead of taking vacations. We might think about that the next time we plan a vacation. Is it possible that these generous doctors knew something we don't about *enjoyment*?

> There are different kinds of gifts, but the same Spirit. There are different kinds of service, but the same Lord. There are different kinds of working, but the same God works all of them in all men. Now to each one the manifestation of the Spirit is given for the common good.
>
> 1 CORINTHIANS 12:4-7, NIV

The Extra Mile

> Only love can transform calculating justice into creative justice. Love makes justice just. Justice without love is always injustice.
>
> PAUL TILLICH

*A*t the ballot box, in the legislative halls, in the courts, and, if need be, on the streets, we must fight those statutes and practices that deny dignity to some or grant special privilege to others. Thanks largely to a massive and compassionate campaign in this country, waged during the past thirty years, many of the more obviously discriminatory laws have been erased from local and state books.

Yet old customs crumble slowly. Old prejudices die hard. Old habits are not easy to break. It has been said that all law floats in a sea of ethics. We are responsible, then, not only for opposing bad laws, but for bringing Christ's Spirit into situations where good law and bad feelings collide.

The Bible teaches that Christians live beyond law. This

means they are to go further than the law. Whereas the law says don't punch your neighbor in the mouth, the Christian ethic says love your neighbor. Even more, love your enemy. Whereas the law says don't run a red light, the Christian ethic says be courteous to the other driver. Be considerate. Whereas the law forces you to go that first mile in your relationships with others, the Christian ethic says go, willingly, that second mile.

> You have heard that it was said, "An eye for an eye and a tooth for a tooth." But I say to you, Do not resist one who is evil. But if any one strikes you on the right cheek, turn to him the other also; and if any one would sue you and take your coat, let him have your cloak as well; and if any one forces you to go one mile, go with him two miles.
>
> MATTHEW 5:38-41, RSV

No Man Is an Island

*D*o you ever feel that in the grand scheme of things, you're pretty much a *nobody*? Do you feel that society would hum along just fine if suddenly you weren't there? In a nation of more than two hundred million people, how important can one individual be? What difference does it make whether I vote or do my job conscientiously? Yet haven't we all read about an election that was decided by a single vote? So let's skip politics and talk about our jobs.

Do you really think a corporation could survive with nothing but big shots? If everybody but the CEOs and the senior managers suddenly disappeared, could the business function? Of course not. Who would file the papers, empty the wastebaskets, answer the phones, and ship the products?

In one game during his rookie season, Chicago Bull Stacey King scored only a single free throw while a teammate named Jordan was totaling sixty-nine points. Later

Stacey said he would always remember it as the night "Michael and I combined for seventy points."

In sports or in business, who gets the most points isn't as important as the final score. That's the sum of everybody's efforts. An army without a general might be inefficient, but a general without an army would be irrelevant. In the battles of life, every soldier counts.

> *The body is a unit, though it is made up of many parts; and though all its parts are many, they form one body. So it is with Christ. . . . The eye cannot say to the hand, "I don't need you!" And the head cannot say to the feet, "I don't need you!" On the contrary, those parts of the body that seem to be weaker are indispensable, and the parts that we think are less honorable we treat with special honor.*
>
> 1 CORINTHIANS 12:12, 21-23, NIV

Application Gap

> Do not merely listen to the word, and so
> deceive yourselves. Do what it says.
>
> JAMES 1:22, NIV

Some people think that most of our problems are a matter of information—that we can solve them if we know enough. Yet most of our problems don't occur because we don't know better. They happen because we don't *do* better.

If knowledge is the answer, everyone who has read a good diet book should be thin. Everyone who has read a book on skiing or tennis or golf should be proficient at those activities.

Clearly, it takes more than knowledge to reach a goal or to solve a problem. Don't get me wrong. I think the "Information Age" is a wonderful thing. But maybe we should start paying more attention to what we already know that we aren't doing.

Just knowing more isn't going to eradicate problems caused by exaggerated egos, greed, selfishness, lethargy, carelessness, or bullheadedness. Information alone won't improve poor attitudes or correct bad actions.

Too often, we're in the same shoes as the old farmer who had listened patiently to an overly enthusiastic salesman who was trying to get him to purchase a thick manual on scientific farming. Finally, the farmer said, "Son, I don't farm half as good as I know how to already." I guess most of us could say the same about how we live.

> Religion consists not in knowing many things, but in practicing the few plain things we know.
>
> JOSEPH GLANVILL

Nothing New on Earth

> Then God said, "Let us make man in our image . . . and let them have dominion over the fish of the sea, and over the birds of the air, and over the cattle, and over all the earth."
>
> GENESIS 1:26, RSV

*W*hat you are about to read comes directly from a report of the United States Commissioner of Patents:

"Great and small cities are fouling watercourses and shorelines with their sewage. The logical solution is to recycle the wastes and obtain valuable fertilizer, while at the same time ending menaces to health."

The expert continues, "After all, the earth is bountiful, but not inexhaustible. And we may not continue to violate with impunity this clearly-indicated law."

The author goes on to document with numerous health statistics and chemical analyses his pleas for an end to pollution.

This sounds like it might have come from this morning's newspaper, doesn't it? But the report is dated 1855. When I first cited this document nearly thirty years ago, Rachel Carson's *Silent Spring* had just reawakened us to the environmental crisis. If the situation was so bad, we wondered, why hadn't someone warned us sooner? The truth is, scores of experts *had* warned us, but we didn't listen.

A lot of dirty water has gone over the dam since 1855. While we are doing better today, we still have much work remaining to fulfill our responsibility to take care of the earth.

> *Action springs not from thought, but from a readiness for responsibility.*
>
> DIETRICH BONHOEFFER

Antidote for Fear

> Courage is being scared to death and saddling up anyway.
>
> JOHN WAYNE

*I*t takes courage to face our world—especially if you're a parent. Besides all the new dangers out there, we've still got all the traditional problems, such as rebellious adolescents. I understand they're coming out with a new teenaged doll this year. You wind it up and it resents you for it.

I once saw this sign on an executive's desk: Confidence is the feeling you have just before you understand the situation. Courage, however, is facing the situation head-on even when you do understand it.

What's your challenge this week? Are you worried your company's merger might leave you without a job? Are you concerned that the doctor may discover your symptom really is something serious? There's plenty to test us: the environment, AIDS, our children's future…. Take courage.

If your courage needs a boost today, try a dose of optimism. I stopped by the ball field to watch my neighbor's son play his first Little League game. His team was behind, eighteen to nothing. I leaned over to him and whispered, "Brad, don't be discouraged by the score."

"Mr. Crim," Brad asked, "why should I be discouraged? We haven't even come up to bat yet."

> Be strong, and let your heart take courage, all you who wait for the Lord!
>
> PSALM 31:24, RSV

Losers and Weepers

> Money is a good servant
> but a bad master.
>
> TRADITIONAL PROVERB

*O*nly once did Jesus tell of a person going to hell. That person was a rich man who let a beggar starve to death at his front door. I doubt Jesus intended this parable as an indictment of all wealthy people, but it does clearly warn that big bank accounts and big hearts don't necessarily share the same owner.

Now there's nothing inherently wrong with money. It can build a hospital, staff a school, or put food in empty stomachs. Yet money can have almost mystical powers over us. For instance, it is reported that when P.T. Barnum died, his very last words were a request to see the day's circus receipts.

It is sad when a person is mastered by money. I once wrote a news story about a man found dead in his tiny shack near a dump. Everyone supposed he had been a pauper. But inside his hovel was discovered nearly $100,000 in cash, squirreled away under a ragged mattress and beneath cracked linoleum. He was so possessed by his possessions that he had refused to buy even the basic necessities.

I know people with fortunes who have lost their sense of values, their sensitivity to others, their friends, and in some cases, their families and their health. True, not all wealthy people have paid such a terrible price, but many have. Those who build monetary empires for their own sake rather than use their resources as channels of concern may end up as losers and weepers.

No servant can serve two masters. Either he will hate the one and love the other, or he will be devoted to the one and despise the other. You cannot serve both God and Money.

LUKE 16:13, NIV

It is not the rich man only who is under the domination of things. They too are slaves who, having no money, are unhappy from the lack of it.

GEORGE MACDONALD

True Grit

> Consider him who endured such opposition
> from sinful men, so that you will not grow
> weary and lose heart.
>
> HEBREWS 12:3, NIV

*J*esus not only defied the laws of the temple and of Rome, but was falsely accused of breaking laws he had not disobeyed. Yet, he spoke not a single word in his own defense or against his accusers. Those who would remove injustice and remodel society would do well to study his firm but generally passive resolve.

It has been argued that Jesus' early followers did not try to correct such abuses as slavery, imperialism, the subjugation of women, and so on. In the words of Ernest Campbell:

Would it not be more accurate to say that those first Christians could not rather than did not try to correct? They were a mere sliver in the Roman Empire. Most of them were slaves. They had no vote, little money, and virtually no political power. But here in these United States millions of citizens profess allegiance to the Judeo-Christian faith. Our situation is markedly different from that which prevailed in the days of Paul and James and Peter. They lived under power. We live with power and in power. We have the numbers to make a difference and thus the responsibility to make that difference. We can't sit down in a barber's chair and ask "What are they doing in Washington?" for we are the they.*

No, we must realize that social action proceeds from our faith. We must oppose those laws and rules that unfairly discriminate, whether *against* a minority of Hispanics or African-Americans or gays, or *for* a minority of corporations with outrageous tax breaks. But opposition doesn't always mean conflict. The persuasive power and ultimate triumph of passive resistance has been proven again and again, from the ministry of Jesus to the effective work of Ghandi and Martin Luther King Jr.

> *Show me your faith apart from your works,*
> *and I by my works will show you my faith.*
> JAMES 2:18, RSV

*Cited in *Presbyterian Life,* January 15, 1969.

Making Molehills Into Mountains

> Young people have enough energy to climb tall mountains of faith, hope, and love. If all we offer them are little molehills, they'll simply go elsewhere for their challenges—to drugs, gangs, cults, and hate.
>
> PAUL LAUER

Today many young people reject the church not because the church has required too much of them, but because it has demanded so little. In my travels around the country, I find American youth bored with a society that's tried to take all the danger out of their lives. Youngsters don't want their lives all plotted out in advance. Many, especially brighter ones, crave an ideal to live for—even one that may cost their lives. Many are ready to trade security for risk.

Idealistic behavior by children can be very upsetting to their more pragmatic parents. Some mothers and fathers find it inconceivable that their offspring should renounce the orderly and safe lives meticulously planned for them. Why should they reject a system that buys comfort with conformity? All that's required of youth is that they hazard no bets—take no chances.

Kids are primed for action. They are ripe for a challenge. They will never buy a religion reduced to a system of thou-shalts and thou-shalt-nots. However, they are attracted to a genuine Christianity that proclaims a compassionate view of life, a view that sees the risks, the possibilities, the golden but perilous promises in the world. For this, in the words of Thomas Howard, is a "wild and elastic and moving world." It's the kind of world where static moral codes alone just won't do.

> Costly grace is the treasure hidden in the field; for the sake of it a man will gladly go and sell all that he has. It is costly because it costs a man his life, and it is grace because it gives a man the only true life.
>
> DIETRICH BONHOEFFER
>
> ❧
>
> Whoever would save his life will lose it; and whoever loses his life for my sake, he will save it.
>
> LUKE 9:24, RSV

The Good Way

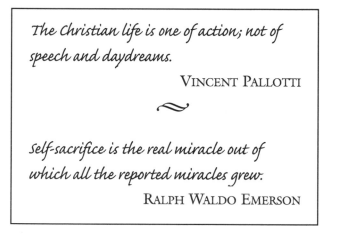

> The Christian life is one of action; not of speech and daydreams.
>
> VINCENT PALLOTTI

> Self-sacrifice is the real miracle out of which all the reported miracles grew.
>
> RALPH WALDO EMERSON

When the Peace Corps was established in 1961, skeptics said it would never work. The Corps promised America's most gifted young people only one reward: a chance to serve. In return for their talents, toil, sweat, and aching muscles, the volunteers were to receive less than the legal minimum wage, less than a part-time bagger in a supermarket could make after school.

The Peace Corps demanded long hours, hard work, and sacrifice. However, the skeptics had overlooked the idealism that had long been cultivated in the minds of American youth. Peace Corps offices were flooded with far more applications than they could process. Today, thirty-eight years later, the Peace Corps has more than seven thousand volunteers working throughout the world, and plans are on the drawing board for even more growth.

A similar kind of challenge attracted people to Jesus. He offered his young disciples no easy life, but they gave up everything to follow him. He promised hardship and predicted death, but they left family, friends, and vocations to answer his call. They gave up the good life to follow his good way: the way of service, the way of sharing, the way of concern—the way of the cross.

> *There is no one who has left house or brothers or sisters or mother or father or children or lands, for my sake and for the gospel, who will not receive a hundredfold now in this time, houses and brothers and sisters and mothers and children and lands, with persecutions, and in the age to come eternal life.*
>
> MARK 10:29-30, RSV

One-Man Vice Squad

How far that little candle throws his beams!
So shines a good deed in a naughty world.
WILLIAM SHAKESPEARE

*U*nited States Customs inspectors are hard to shock. They've seen just about everything. But the guys who keep an eagle eye on traffic across the United States/Mexico border were not quite prepared for the bizarre case of "nonsmuggling" they ran into when an American showed up on the Mexican side with ninety-three pounds of marijuana! He didn't try to hide it. In fact, he declared it! Then he told Customs officials he had deliberately purchased the pot in Mexico just so it could be kept off the American market and out of the hands of his fourteen children.

The man apparently didn't want any publicity. He asked that his name not be released. However, Customs officials did check out his story. After confirming it, all they could do was say thank you and let the man cross back to the United States.

That ninety-three pounds of pot would have brought thousands of dollars on the streets of America's cities. Officials don't know what the nonsmuggler paid for it. Apparently, somebody forgot to tell that one-man vice squad that individuals don't count anymore.

> *Neither do men light a candle, and put it under a bushel, but on a candlestick; and it giveth light unto all that are in the house. Let your light so shine before men, that they may see your good works, and glorify your Father which is in heaven.*
>
> MATTHEW 5:15-16, KJV

The Promise of Freedom

Christianity promises to make men free. It never promises to make them independent.

W.R. INGE

*O*nce the great violinist Fritz Kreisler was approached backstage by an enthusiastic fan who cried, "Oh, Mr. Kreisler, I'd give my life to play as you do."

Quietly he replied, "Madam, I did." Kreisler was free to perform masterpieces in a magnificent way, but not because he merely declared his freedom to do so. It was because he understood that freedom to do as he pleased with a violin meant he first had to learn the rules and submit to the rigorous discipline of music.

Personal success, no less than scientific or artistic success, depends upon acceptance of this principle that truth and training are cornerstones of freedom. Freedom from self depends upon recognition of how enslaved we are. No one can become free who believes he is inherently free. Any expert on alcoholism will tell you that the first step alcoholics must take on the road back to rehabilitation is to fully admit their problem. They must face the truth about their condition. Only as they begin to understand why they drink can they begin to conquer the compulsion.

Freedom comes from cooperation with the laws of life. It is not the product of opposition to them. If we were to devise an equation for stating freedom in mathematical terms, it probably would be: Knowledge plus discipline equals freedom.

> *Liberty, rightly understood, is an inestimable blessing, but liberty without wisdom and without justice is no better than wild and savage licentiousness.*
>
> CHANCELLOR KENT
>
> *Live as free men, but do not use your freedom as a cover-up for evil; live as servants of God.*
>
> 1 PETER 2:16, NIV

The Freedom Process

> *If you continue in my word, you are truly my disciples, and you will know the truth, and the truth will make you free.*
>
> JOHN 8:31-32, RSV

As a broadcaster I hope I am more free today—from prejudice, incompetence, fear, and timidity—than I was a year ago. I believe I am experiencing progressively greater freedom to be a good commentator. I do not now, nor do I ever expect to, claim absolute freedom as a journalist, for I will always be constrained both by external pressures and by internal inadequacies. Still, I can constantly cultivate and accelerate the freedom process within myself.

As a Christian I hope I am more free today—of self-centeredness, vengefulness, apathy, and insensitivity—than I was a year ago. I believe I am finding greater freedom to be a whole person. I am not now, nor do I expect in this life to be, absolutely free, because my moral capacities are limited and my motives are not always pure. However, I can move steadily along the path of renewal and reform toward that final freedom that all Christians believe will be ultimately theirs. For, as the late Roy Burkhart put it, the ultimate freedom is the freedom from death.

> We shall be outwardly free when we
> unbind ourselves from slavery within.
>
> NIKOLAY BERDYAYEV

Now Hear This

*I*t was one of those small, personal experiences that seemed to reflect one of the world's big problems. While we were waiting for our food at a carry out restaurant, the girl behind the counter called off a number, customers glanced at their tickets, but no one moved forward. The girl called out another number. Then another. There was still no response. She was frustrated, and the customers obviously irritated, as unclaimed orders stacked up on the counter. Finally, somebody figured out that the numbering system had somehow gone wrong. The customers' checks didn't match the numbers on the orders.

The incident shows what can happen when communications break down: confusion, chaos, anger, and, of course, a complete halt to progress and efficiency. In this case, there was no production trouble. The food was coming out of the kitchen right on schedule. There was no lack of good intentions. The girl wanted to serve the customers—and they wanted to be served. It was just that the two sides didn't understand each other. They weren't speaking the same language. The system was stopped dead.

> *Unless you speak intelligible words with your tongue, how will anyone know what you are saying? You will just be speaking into the air. Undoubtedly there are all sorts of languages in the world, yet none of them is without meaning. If then I do not grasp the meaning of what someone is saying, I am a foreigner to the speaker, and he is a foreigner to me.*
>
> 1 CORINTHIANS 14:9-11, NIV

Simple and Direct

> We can examine what goes into our
> mouths, why not what comes out of them
> as well?
>
> JOHN BONA

"Jargon" is one of the biggest barriers to clear communication. Every profession has it. Doctors, lawyers, journalists, and, yes, even Christians, tend to use words that may be meaningful only to them.

If you heard me say, "Dolly in one, set up two on a two-shot, and stand by three for a CU of the guest," you might wonder what language I was speaking. Actually, I'd be speaking television language. While any producer—or stagehand—would know exactly what the phrases meant, someone unfamiliar with what goes on in a TV studio might not get it.

Jargon can interfere with our attempts to communicate God's love for the world. Jesus certainly understood that. Remember how he condemned the ostentatious jargon of the Pharisee's prayer? This very religious man surely knew all the right words. No doubt he'd mastered the ecclesiastical jargon. But he was using this "inside language" to show off. He was putting his piety on display.

The prayer that received Jesus' approval was the simple, straightforward plea of the publican who had some guilt he needed to get off his chest.

In the most uncomplicated terms, this tortured soul said simply that he had sinned, and he asked God to show him mercy.

What I call "church-speak" may impress other Christians. The jargon may be as familiar to them as television terms are to me. Yet if we really want to communicate—if our goal is to share the Good News that God loves us—then we need to examine our words from time to time. Remember: It's not what we say that matters. It's what the other person hears.

Let your conversation be always full of grace, seasoned with salt, so that you may know how to answer everyone.

COLOSSIANS 4:6, NIV

Colorblind

> Unless you turn and become like children, you will never enter the kingdom of heaven.
>
> MATTHEW 18:3, RSV

*I*srael J. Ward worked at a suburban department store in Louisville, Kentucky.

Once, Israel was walking down an aisle between two counters when he heard a little girl call to him.

"Mister, is this your little boy?" she asked.

At first, Ward wasn't sure the child was speaking to him. She appeared to be about four years old. She was holding by the hand a small boy, two or three years old.

Again she called to Mr. Ward, this time looking him straight in the eye.

"Mister, I said, is this your little boy? He seems to be lost."

Israel Ward said, "No, young lady, I'm afraid that's not my little boy."

Just about that time, the lost boy's mother came for him.

But the brief experience made a lasting impression on Ward. You see, the little lost boy and the little girl were both white. Israel Ward is black. He will never forget the little "color-blind" girl who had not yet been taught to tell the difference.

> God is only father in the sense of father of all. When I hate someone or deny that God is his father—it is not he who loses, but me; for then I have no father.
>
> SØREN KIERKEGAARD

Words Can Kill

> *A man who is possessed by fear always begins to persecute.*
>
> NIKOLAY BERDYAYEV

*G*enuine commitment can be guaranteed to make people uncomfortable. It is disconcerting to be around someone whose motives seem higher, purer than your own. It is humiliating to have your darkness penetrated by the brilliance of someone's idealism. Throughout history, lesser men have sought to extinguish such lights. For instance, in Jesus' day, the Pharisees were determined to cut this spiritual superman down to size. When they could not, they conspired to kill him. Those who have taken seriously his challenges have been risking death ever since.

There are many ways to kill a person. The modern believer in America usually doesn't face physical death, although the rise of hate groups and racial violence is a matter of growing concern. However, the contemporary Christian does confront the very real possibility of character assassination, and sometimes a word can be mightier than a sword.

No argument sufficiently counters a charge like "Everybody's got an angle." But I see that accusation refuted every day in dozens of small, and sometimes large, ways. I see people demonstrating authentic decency in routine encounters. I know people who, unquestionably, are motivated by compassion and love.

> If the world hates you, know that it has hated me before it hated you. . . . Remember the word that I said to you, "A servant is not greater than his master." If they persecuted me, they will persecute you.
>
> JOHN 15:18, 20, RSV

Boomerang Encouragement

> A cheerful look brings joy to the heart, and
> good news gives health to the bones.
>
> PROVERBS 15:30, NIV

*G*reeting cards are wonderful things. Often when traveling I'll discover a card tucked into my suitcase with a loving message from my wife, Renee. This is an important reminder that she cares.

Writer Robert Veninga tells of a woman so depressed over the holidays that she was considering suicide. Then she received a Christmas card from her boss. He had no clue that this woman was so discouraged, but on the card he had written, "I don't know what we would do without you. Thanks for being so competent, so helpful."

That woman framed the card and put it up in her kitchen. She said it was like getting a sign that proclaimed, "You're going to make it."

Author Alex Haley was no overnight success. For years he received one rejection notice after another. Usually they were standard, printed forms. One day an editor sent him a rejection slip with a handwritten notation on it: "Nice try." Haley says he almost cried. That little note told him someone out there had actually read his manuscript.

No matter how powerless we may feel on any given day, we all possess an incredible power to encourage. The strange thing is, we can't brighten someone else's day without revitalizing our own. Spreading encouragement is like tossing confetti. Inevitably some of it is going to blow back on us.

He who refreshes others will himself be refreshed.

PROVERBS 11:25, NIV

The Social Good News

> *If justice prevails, good faith is found in treaties, truth in transactions, order in government, the earth is at peace, and heaven itself sheds over us its beneficent light and radiates down to us its blessed influence.*
>
> J.B. BOSSUET

What our cities require is a moral revolution, the kind Jesus preached. His was, after all, the first really revolutionary concept to come along in centuries. Long before his birth, many thinkers dreamed of Utopia and had pondered the possibility of restructuring society.

Jesus went far beyond that. He did not deny the need for social change. He endorsed it. But Jesus told us that people can change—that human nature can be transformed. Love can replace hate. Generosity can overcome greed. Jesus' renewed society was to be built with new people, not merely new conditions.

Some still argue whether Christ came to save individuals

or to save society. It is a senseless argument because the two objectives are inseparable. Jesus clearly came to change individuals *and* to revolutionize the way they relate to each other.

There would be little logic in debating whether the medical community is responsible for the health of individuals or for the health of the nation. How can the two be contradictory? They are complementary.

Of course the medical profession is concerned with healing individuals. Yet when problems such as AIDS, cigarette smoking, or air pollution endanger large numbers of people, we then speak of a *national* health problem. Mass inoculations, citywide health campaigns, and national drives against disease never contradict medicine's responsibility to the individual.

So, too, Christianity must speak not only to the soul and intellect of individuals, but to the great social issues of the day as well.

> Put them all away: anger, wrath, malice, slander, and foul talk from your mouth. Do not lie to one another, seeing that you have put off the old nature with its practices and have put on the new nature, which is being renewed in knowledge after the image of its creator.
>
> COLOSSIANS 3:8-10, RSV

Remembering Newark

> Returning violence for violence multiplies violence, adding deeper darkness to a night already devoid of stars.
>
> MARTIN LUTHER KING JR.

I can never forget my assignment in Newark. It was on a long, hot night in July 1967. That steaming, poverty-plagued city had exploded in violence. ABC had sent me to cover what history would record as "The Newark Riots."

I remember lying flat on the sticky pavement of Springfield Avenue as police and sniper bullets whined overhead. For nearly twenty minutes we were pinned down by the continuous blaze of gunfire.

That night, I saw a fireman shot in the face. I watched him die.

I talked with a young girl whose mother had been killed by a police bullet while she watched television inside their tenement.

I saw anger and alienation in the eyes of young blacks;

anguish and despair in the eyes of the old; fear and distrust in the faces of children.

I remember the expressions of policemen and National Guardsmen. Their eyes transmitted a discordant symphony of emotions, from frustration to hatred. There was little evidence of compassion or understanding on either side of the black-white line that divided an oppressed minority and an insensitive majority.

I prayed for Newark that night. I saw some pretty tough guys—police-beat reporters, hard-nosed city hall types—get lumps in their throats as they gazed into the decaying entrails of a ghetto. Some of them looked as though they might be praying, too.

I do not remember the exact words, but I was thinking, *Father, forgive them. They don't know what they're doing. Forgive the looter. Forgive the sniper. Forgive the policeman. Forgive all these children of yours who are hating each other tonight. Forgive all of us for not having cared enough.*

> *Father, forgive them; for they know not what they do.*
>
> LUKE 23:34, RSV

All Things Being Equal

> *There is neither Jew nor Greek, slave nor free, male nor female, for you are all one in Christ Jesus.*
>
> GALATIANS 3:28, NIV

*I*n most public schools, middle- and upper-middle-class children score higher and perform better than youngsters at the lower end of the economic scale. Also, in most public schools, the poorer children tend to be nonwhites. These two facts have led some social critics to conclude that African-Americans are intellectually inferior to white children, that their learning potential is lower.

Well, the two facts just don't add up that way. It's also a fact that learning potential is related to socioeconomic conditions, and youngsters from deprived backgrounds consistently do worse in school than affluent children—whatever their color.

Blaming poor performance on inherent deficiencies is too easy and lets us off the hook. Change the structure of society, so that African-Americans can break out of their isolation and into the economic mainstream, and you'll change the educational performance of African-American children. But it will also benefit white kids.

My grandchildren need to learn this lesson as much as any African-American child does: Racial prejudice is a contagious disease that ravages and distorts the minds of all it infects—regardless of their color.

> We are confronted primarily with a moral issue. It is as old as the Scriptures and is as clear as the American Constitution. The heart of the question is whether all Americans are to be afforded equal rights and equal opportunities. We face, therefore, a moral crisis as a country and as a people.
>
> JOHN F. KENNEDY

Real Self-Help

> There are eight rungs in charity. The highest is when you help a man to help himself.
>
> MAIMONIDES

*I*t took riots to focus media attention on some of the good things happening in Los Angeles neighborhoods. One of those good things is the *Food From the Hood* program, a student-owned business that started out with just a few acres under cultivation. Now it sells three kinds of salad dressing, has an outlet in New York selling flavored applesauce, and soon will have franchises in Hawaii, Chicago, and Philadelphia.

What is *Food From the Hood*? It's a way for high school students to get into business and earn money for college. Students earn anywhere from $2,000 to $3,000 a year, which is put into a trust fund. So far, a total of more than $110,000 has been earned, and all but three of the program's sixty-six graduates are now in college, with the other three planning to go.

Yet *Food From the Hood* does more than enable students

to earn money. It also provides tutoring, preparation for the SAT exams, and a tour of historically African-American colleges. It teaches young people about business; about responsibility; about opportunity and what can happen when a person works hard to realize a dream.

As the *Food From the Hood* program shows, some gardens can produce a rich harvest of personal growth.

> We . . . urge you, brothers, to go on making even greater progress and to make a point of living quietly, attending to your own business and earning your living, just as we told you to, so that you may earn the respect of outsiders and not be dependent on anyone.
>
> 1 THESSALONIANS 4:10-11, NJB

An Affirmative Negative

> Just say no!
>
> CONTEMPORARY SLOGAN
>
> ⤮
>
> What part of the word "no" don't you understand?
>
> COUNTRY SONG

I'm not one of those people who blames all society's ills upon so-called permissiveness. I'm not sure I even know what that term means. However, it does seem to me that all of us could learn to use the word *no* better than we do. Most of us have been taught all of our lives, either explicitly or by implication, that yes is good, no is bad. Think positive. Eliminate everything from your life that's negative. Maybe all this emphasis upon the affirmative has turned us into a bunch of yes-men and -women.

This came home to me personally some time ago when a friend and colleague suggested that perhaps I was accepting too many speaking invitations. Pointing out the risks to health, happiness, and family life that are incurred by overextension, this friend said, "Mort, you really need to learn how to say no."

It's a most useful word, whether we're confronting a *personal* question, such as how best to invest our time, an *environmental* decision, such as how much soot and sewage we're going to let industry pump into our air and water, or a *moral* choice, such as whether we're going to cheat on our taxes or on our spouse.

There are times when the ability to give a negative answer is a positive virtue.

You will always have joy in the evening if you spend the day fruitfully.

THOMAS À KEMPIS

Selfless Self-Interest

> In everything, do to others what you would
> have them do to you.
>
> MATTHEW 7:12, NIV

*W*ould you like to know how to get almost anyone to do almost anything you want?

Lois told her best friend, Jennifer, that she had decided to marry Tom. Jennifer was shocked. "But Lois, you've always told me that when you're with Fred, you think he's the greatest person in the world."

"That's true," Lois admitted. "But when I'm with Tom, he makes me think *I'm* the greatest person in the world."

There you have it—the secret of getting your way, whether you're dealing with a reluctant love interest, a difficult boss, or an obstinate child. In the end, it's your concern for the other person's needs that brings that person around.

The best and most satisfying successes I've experienced in my career and personal life have been those where everybody wins, not where I had to succeed at somebody else's expense.

In all of life's encounters, we all want to know "What's in it for me?" The person who can put the needs of others at the center of the equation comes out ahead in the long run.

Harry Truman once said that he had learned that the best way to give advice to your children is to find out what they want and advise them to do it.

Appeals to self-interest can be quite convincing, as in the case of some parachute packers during World War II. These workers had a dismal record. Nineteen out of twenty chutes weren't opening. This was not good.

The manager discovered that by requiring the packers to personally test their parachutes by jumping from a plane, quality rose to 100 percent.

I lose God, I lose the world, I lose myself, if I want only to clutch at things and use them only for my own pleasure or profit.

GERALD VANN

Cherries or Pits?

> The standing miracle of this visible world is little thought of, yet when we arouse ourselves to contemplate it, it is a greater miracle than the rarest and most unheard-of marvels.
>
> AUGUSTINE

For some, life's a bowl of cherries. For others, it's the pits. How do we keep our sanity with so much chaos all around us? How do we maintain emotional balance in a world that seems sometimes out of control?

There are several ways of dealing with this dilemma:

There's the chameleon approach. We have these little lizards in our yard in Florida. They're able to change colors almost instantly. If they're on a leaf, they turn green. On concrete, they become gray. Some people are like that, always reflecting their environment. Like the chameleon, they have no real convictions. If life's good for them, that's all that matters.

There's the ostrich approach. Some people bury their heads in the sand. Psychologists call this "denial." Just pretend all's right with the world. Forget the hatred and the horror. Tune it out. What you don't see can't hurt you.

Lizard-types are rarely happy, because they never know who they are. They're victims of their surroundings.

Ostrich-types are rarely fulfilled, because they never come to terms with the adventures of existence. While they're oblivious to life's evils, they also miss all its wonder, excitement, and opportunity.

Happiness and fulfillment are found only when we pull our heads out of the sand and see life with all its richness and diversity; when we develop character of our own so that instead of merely taking on the color of our surroundings, we make our environment a reflection of ourselves.

Look into the bowl and you'll see that it contains both cherries and pits.

> *The only work of which we are absolute masters, the only one that we can encompass in a glance, and organize, concerns our own heart.*
>
> FRANÇOIS MAURIAC

Love Goes Deep

> It is only the souls that do not love that go empty in this world.
>
> ROBERT HUGH BENSON

William G. King Sr. is a man whose love goes deep. King is white. His son, William King Jr., a Marine, was murdered in Washington, D.C. Three African-Americans were charged with the killing. The response of the elder King was to request an integrated honor guard for his son's funeral. He said, "My wife and I feel that the time has come when we have to stand up as individuals ... for understanding and harmony. Somebody has to make the first step."

King went on to say, "I've been able to wash out of my mind and heart any animosity toward people black or white. I have no desire for revenge."

Dixie Whitted's love also goes deep. Her husband, Martin, was killed by four teenagers as he drove his bus through the Hunters Point section of San Francisco. Widowed at the age of thirty, Mrs. Whitted requested that gifts in honor of her slain husband be given to a memorial fund for youth work in Hunters Point. She said, "I want this experience to be a way of helping the minorities of our city."

The measure of Christian love is not how much we love those who love us, but rather how deeply we can feel for those who seem to love us least.

Love your enemies, do good to those who hate you, bless those who curse you, pray for those who abuse you. To him who strikes you on the cheek, offer the other also; and from him who takes away your coat do not withhold even your shirt.

If you love those who love you, what credit is that to you? For even sinners love those who love them.

LUKE 6:27-29, 32, RSV

Believing Is Seeing

> *If only for this life we have hope in Christ,*
> *we are to be pitied more than all men.*
>
> 1 CORINTHIANS 15:19, NIV

*T*he words *I believe* have a special quality when they are spoken with conviction. They affirm an absolute faith in the future, a faith invulnerable to the fears of the moment. They fling confidence into the face of terror and tragedy. They tenderly pour compassion and care over a world of war, starvation, and frustration.

In an era when people suffocate under the smog of hopelessness and despair, those who have found faith breathe the clean, exhilarating air of assurance. They know the future is not in the hands of some fickle fate, some blind and mindless whim. They know that all things, ultimately and finally, are working together toward good.

The apostle Paul once said that the committed person who has hope only in this life is a most miserable person. His noblest dreams will evaporate and his finest works will turn to dust.

An alternative to such despair was handed to us hundreds of years ago on a small hillside just outside the ancient city of Jerusalem. There a symbol of one man's death became the symbol of all our hopes. There a cross was erected. A young man was hanged on it, and the world was never again the same.

> And we know that in all things God works for the good of those who love him, who have been called according to his purpose.
>
> ROMANS 8:28, NIV

Best Friends

> You cannot imagine how much I love you
> when I see you suffering. If only someone
> could arrange for me to see you and let me
> put my arms around your neck, the way a
> little boy hangs on to his dear father.
>
> ANTHONY CLARET

*A*nimals have long played an important role in human health. For instance, potent drugs are always tested first on animals. But now some animals are playing a more personal role. In Salt Lake City, TURN Community Services has employed a German Shepherd named Grizzly to help autistic children connect with other humans.

So far the experiment is promising. Justin, like most children afflicted with autism, often appears to be daydreaming. He can seem withdrawn and have little or no recognition of the people around him. At first the boy seemed to resent Grizzly and stepped on his paw. But by the eighth session, boy and dog had made an obvious connection. Justin was less agitated and even allowed Grizzly to eat food from his hand.

It's long been known that the elderly—especially the lonely and those suffering Alzheimer's—do better with pets in their lives. Why do dogs and cats prove to be such good friends to those with special needs? Perhaps because pets don't ask questions, they forgive easily, and they never criticize.

A dog seems to understand what people frequently miss: the value of *just being there*. Strange what an animal can teach us about being human.

> *Clothe yourselves with compassion, kindness, humility, meekness, and patience. Bear with one another and, if anyone has a complaint against another, forgive each other.*
>
> COLOSSIANS 3:12-13, NRSV

Just a Little Mercy

*T*his is the story of a meter maid who may have done her job too well.

In Knoxville, Tennessee, a pickup truck was parked outside the post office building. The man and woman who owned the old truck were inside the Salvation Army office next door, picking up some badly needed clothing and bedding for themselves and their ten children. The ten children, ragged and obviously poor, were in the back of the truck, waiting for their parents, when along came the local meter maid. She put a ticket on the truck's windshield.

Some federal employees, inside the post office, saw what had happened. One of them went out, took the ticket off the truck, and wrote a letter to the police chief. The letter explained how furious the workers were at the meter maid for her lack of sensitivity. It went on to say, "If you feel this ticket must be paid, return it to us and we'll pay it immediately."

No doubt the meter maid felt she was only doing her job of enforcing the law. However, the federal workers felt it was a case where *justice* needed to be tempered by *mercy*.

> The more merciful acts you do, the more mercy you will receive.
>
> WILLIAM PENN

The Beauty Remains

Consider it pure joy, my brothers, whenever you face trials of many kinds, because you know that the testing of your faith develops perseverance.

JAMES 1:2-3, NIV

Some people suspect women handle pain better than men. I believe it. When it comes to being sick, I'm a wimp compared to my wife. She's a real trooper. A day after surgery, Renee went grocery shopping, ran errands, and put in half a day at her office. I would have expected more time off with a bad cold.

Renee believes necessity, not genetics, produces this unequal capacity. Women, she reasons, are better at pushing on beyond their pain because they've had to. Traditionally, women have been so busy taking care of the family's needs, they've had little time to fuss over their own aches and hurts.

Certainly a strong sense of responsibility can help push us beyond our pain. Barbara Walters' interview with Henry

Mancini shortly before his death from cancer revealed him still composing music. His face and his hands showed the suffering, but his strong creative drive transcended it.

Artist Auguste Renoir was almost paralyzed by arthritis during the last ten years of his life. Still, he continued to paint. His younger artist friend Henri Matisse watched Renoir struggling in his studio one day, fighting tortuous pain with each brush stroke.

"Auguste," he said, "why do you continue to paint when you are in such agony?"

Renoir answered, simply, "The beauty remains. The pain passes."

> *It is impossible that anything, however small, suffered for God's sake, should fail to meet with its reward.*
>
> THOMAS À KEMPIS

Thinking About Death

> When we come to realize that death that crushes is but the tender clasp of God that loves, it loses all its terrors.
>
> VINCENT MCNABB

*T*he fact of death seems more visible and more constant today than ever before. Newspaper headlines describe how a tornado ruins in a minute the town it took a century to build. Radio and television newscasts remind us of our mortality with casualty figures from floods, plane crashes, highway accidents, and wars. Heart attacks, cancer, AIDS, and countless other maladies continue their grim reaping. Death is one certainty no one questions.

The problem is that most people have not resolved the ultimate question posed by death. They know only that they must die. A psychiatrist friend of mine tells me that no one enjoys complete mental health who has not come to terms with death.

Dag Hammarskjöld once observed that in the last analysis, it is our conception of death that decides our answers to all the major questions of life. So what you or I believe about the grave greatly influences who we are. Our view of the hereafter profoundly influences our actions in the here and now.

It is difficult to walk purposefully and confidently through life if one shares, for instance, Bertrand Russell's depressing view of life and death. Human beings are nothing, he said, "but the product of accidental colocations of atoms. All the noonday brightness of human genius is destined to ultimate extinction." Sadly, Russell speaks for millions of people today.

Hear another voice, however—a voice telling how it can be. Martin Luther King Jr. said of death: "We need not fear it. The God who brought our whirling planet from primal vapor and has led the human pilgrimage for lo these many centuries can most assuredly lead us through death's dark night into the bright daybreak of eternal life."

> *Death has been swallowed up in victory.*
> *Where, O death, is your victory?*
> *Where, O death, is your sting?*
> 1 CORINTHIANS 15:54-55, NIV

Talk About Death

*T*here was a time when people openly discussed death, and even mentioning the word *sex* was regarded as obscene. Now, it's the other way around! Sex is openly discussed in our society, but we are mum about death.

This silence has serious implications for those who are dying. They may wish to discuss it with their families or friends, but often can't find anyone willing to listen. You see, we've tried to pretend death docsn't happen. Yet, failing to face up to it merely complicates the problem posed by death.

Anthropologist Margaret Mead said that many of our anxieties result from the fact that no matter how many other problems we might banish someday—hunger, violence, or whatever—we know we can never banish death.

Facing this fact can help us to make the right choices and

to use wisely the limited time available to us. Trying to ignore death can bind us up with a thousand useless worries. Since death is every bit as much a part of life as sex, it deserves at least as much attention.

We shun the thought of death as sad, but death will only be sad to those who have not thought of it. It must come sooner or later, and then he who has refused to seek the truth in life will be forced to face it in death.

FRANÇOIS FÉNELON

Teach us to number our days aright,
That we may gain a heart of wisdom.

PSALM 90:12, NIV

Release

Like a seafarer on deserted waters who looks to the stars, choose ideals as your guides. And following them, you will reach your destiny.

CARL SCHURZ

*T*he news report was datelined Biloxi, Mississippi.

A young woman—a professional dancer—tired of living, had tried to end her life by jumping from a dock.

Nearby, a young man saw the splash, heard the woman thrashing around in the water, took off his jacket, and jumped in. However, he had forgotten one small detail— he didn't know how to swim.

Well, when the woman saw her would-be rescuer gulping water and going under, she suddenly forgot her problems and swam over to save him. As she dragged him ashore, it felt as though she were leaving her own despair in the water. She would later tell authorities that, faced with another person's crisis, her life had—if only for that moment—taken on a purpose, something it did not have before.

According to the news account, she was taken to the hospital, treated for exposure, and then released. But her *real* release had occurred when she had discovered a reason to live.

There's no more important decision we'll ever make than determining our purpose in life. After all, if we don't know where we're going, we're likely to end up where we're headed.

> Greater love has no one than this, that one lay down his life for his friends.
>
> JOHN 15:13, NIV
>
> ∼
>
> The highest flights of charity, devotion, trust, patience, bravery, to which the wings of human nature have spread themselves have been flown for religious ideals.
>
> WILLIAM JAMES

Traveling Light

> There is an art of simplicity. It will need no end of thinking out and it is worth learning.
>
> TEMPLE GAIRDNER

"One of these days we'll learn that we don't have to take so much," said my wife, Renee, as she tossed our suitcases onto the bed. It's true, we always overpack. Inevitably we bring back clothing we didn't wear and didn't need.

I should have learned the lesson years ago, after my luggage was lost on a flight to Uruguay. I had been assigned to cover a four-day presidential summit conference, and somehow I managed to get through the entire event with only the essentials I had carried in my briefcase and the suit I was wearing.

In a sense, our days are like suitcases. Yet, unlike suitcases, our days are all the same size. We don't get to choose whether we'll take one or two, small or large. Each of us is given a twenty-four-hour day. It's up to us how we fill it.

Just as with suitcases, some people pack their days more wisely than others. Some have a knack for figuring out what's essential and what they can do without. And when emergencies disrupt our carefully planned schedules, we discover that a lot of stuff we considered necessary ... isn't.

When filling your suitcase or your calendar, ask this question about each item: What's the worst thing that may happen if I leave it out? An honest answer will allow you to travel through life a lot lighter.

And why do you worry about clothes? See how the lilies of the field grow. They do not labor or spin. Yet I tell you that not even Solomon in all his splendor was dressed like one of these. If that is how God clothes the grass of the field, which is here today and tomorrow is thrown into the fire, will he not much more clothe you, O you of little faith?

MATTHEW 6:28-30, NIV

Finding the Meaning

> *This most elegant system of suns, planets and comets could only arise from the purpose and sovereignty of an intelligent and mighty being. He rules them all, not as a soul of the world, but a sovereign Lord of all things.*
>
> ISAAC NEWTON

lbert Einstein was only four or five years old when he watched the motion of a compass needle and said, "Something deeply hidden has to be behind things." Einstein never lost his faith in creative purpose. In fact, as he grew to manhood and began exploring the mysteries of the universe, that faith grew. In later life, Einstein said: "My religion consists of a humble admiration for the Superior Spirit who reveals himself in the slight details we are able to perceive with our frail and feeble minds." For Einstein, life was a symmetry of significance.

Most of history's heroes have been men and women

with deep convictions about the ultimate meaning of existence. One need not, however, be a moral giant to discover meaning. One need only confront life with intellectual honesty, humility, and sensitivity.

Why is sensitivity important? Because there are so many subtle expressions of meaning woven into the fabric of life. These intimations of ultimate purpose do not beat upon our intellects with the force of a hurricane. Rather, they stir softly, like a refreshing breeze, across the acrid pessimism of our day.

> The Lord passed by, and a great and strong wind rent the mountains, and broke in pieces the rocks before the Lord, but the Lord was not in the wind; and after the wind an earthquake, but the Lord was not in the earthquake; and after the earthquake a fire, but the Lord was not in the fire; and after the fire a still small voice. And when Elijah heard it, he wrapped his face in his mantle and went out and stood at the entrance of the cave.
>
> 1 KINGS 19:11-13, RSV

A Reason for Hope

> Only faith in a life after death ... can give consolation.
>
> WINSTON S. CHURCHILL

Ron was only thirty years old when doctors told him that his kidney disease, and the diabetes that caused it, would be fatal. At the age of thirty-three, Ron lay dying in a Minneapolis hospital. By this time he was blind, his body ridden with pain. But Ron told his young wife, Karen, he was ready to die.

In an interview with a columnist for the *Minneapolis Star*, Ron said: "I tell you I'm not afraid of death. Do you know how I feel? I'm kind of excited. Some time ago I became what I think is a real Christian. I now really believe this is just a beginning."

Some may be quick to regard such optimism as a false sense of security, evolved from fear. A skeptic may see in such deathbed confidence only the fantasizing of a desperate man, assurance born of a wish rather than of reason.

True, you can't achieve such confidence strictly by reasoning. Yet neither does such tranquillity come simply by wishing for it. Christianity does appeal to the human intellect. For example, reason acknowledges that love is better than hate, that hope is better than despair, that life is better than death. Christianity also has an emotional appeal, for our desire for survival is one of our strongest feelings. But it wasn't wish and reason alone that powered Ron's confidence. The secret of his assurance was his Christian faith, a belief that gathered up his desire and logic and transfused them with hope.

> Now this is eternal life: that they may know you, the only true God, and Jesus Christ, whom you have sent.
>
> JOHN 17:3, NIV

To Tell the Truth

Divine Providence has granted this gift to man—that those things which are honest are also the most advantageous.

QUINTILIAN

"*H*onesty is the best policy" is an old saying. But is this true in the real world? Is truthfulness really good for business?

John Wanamaker thought so. The old department store tycoon used to have an advertising man who *always* told the truth. He simply refused to write an ad that wasn't honest.

Once Wanamaker's was about to offer some neckties for the unbelievable price of twenty-five cents. Even in those days that was incredibly cheap. However, after this adman examined the ties, he decided they really weren't very good, so this is what he wrote for his ad: "They're not as good as they look—but they're good enough for twenty-five cents."

Guess what? Those ties sold so fast the store had to keep

buying them for the next several weeks to keep up with demand.

Is honesty good for business? Customers think so. And what works in business works in our relationships. It was Mark Twain who advised, "When in doubt, tell the truth."

We all prefer to deal with those we can trust. In a society where fudging the facts seems to be a national pastime, it's up to each of us to fight truth decay.

> *Truth makes the devil blush.*
>
> THOMAS FULLER

No Excuses

We have forty million reasons for failure,
but not a single excuse.

RUDYARD KIPLING

*A*fter hearing a news report about a burglar, five-year-old Tommy asked, "Mommy, what's a second story man?" She said, "Your dad's one. If I don't believe his first story, he's always got a second one." For some people, life is a daily struggle to cover their backsides, excuse their failings, or explain away their faults. Wouldn't it be more productive to invest the same energy and ingenuity into achievement instead of alibi? Helen Keller, one of the most inspiring and accomplished women of the twentieth century, could neither see nor hear. She had a wonderful excuse for inaction. Yet her contributions to society were awesome.

Ray Charles could have used his blindness as an excuse for failure, but Ray was too busy writing and recording his incomparable music to waste time on alibis. A man with a serious spinal deformity invented the radio. The mirror you looked into this morning was perfected by a man who couldn't hear.

Heather Whitestone certainly had an excuse for giving up her dream of becoming Miss America. No physically disabled person had ever won the crown. Yet Heather wasn't interested in alibis. So a nation was brought to tears by a beautiful ballet routine, performed to music the ballerina could not hear. But she *could* make us *listen*. Her message was clear: It's not our disabilities that handicap us. It's our excuses.

Every person feels instinctively that all the beautiful sentiments in the world weigh less than a single lovely action.

JAMES RUSSELL LOWELL

Through faith we experience the meaning of the world. Through action we give it meaning.

LEO BAECK

Rhetoric or Results?

> Those who do what is true come to the
> light, so that it may be clearly seen that
> their deeds have been done in God.
>
> JOHN 3:21, NRSV

*I*f words were dollars, Congress would produce enough in one session to wipe out the national debt. This is not to suggest that words don't matter. They matter a great deal. Every great or noble thought must be expressed in words before we can convert it into action.

But Congress isn't the only place where they know how to filibuster: Too often, instead of becoming road maps toward realization, words become substitutes for our actions. As Liza Doolittle put it in *My Fair Lady,* "If you're in love, show me." In that delightful musical comedy, Liza finally expresses the universal exasperation we feel when promise isn't backed by performance.

How much further along America would be right now if we were acting upon the millions of words printed in thousands of reports created by hundreds of commissions to analyze scores of society's problems. For the most part, they remain just words.

Our children like to hear us say we love them, but a hundred loving words are no substitute for a single act of caring. Our boss or our spouse may enjoy hearing us expound on some great project we plan to pursue, but without action, the words are hollow.

Sometimes words actually get in the way, as they might have in the following instance. During the early sixties, my father was working quietly and effectively with other community leaders in his hometown to extend equal rights to black citizens. As a journalist, I saw potential in his work for a national news story, and suggested it. "Son," my dad said, "I don't want publicity. I want results."

> *The Christian ideal has not been tried and found wanting. It has been found difficult and left untried.*
>
> G.K. CHESTERTON

Love Letters

> I, Paul, write this greeting with my own hand. ... My love be with you all in Christ Jesus.
>
> 1 CORINTHIANS 16:21, 24, RSV

A lot of money, time, and talent are being invested in the wars on killer diseases such as AIDS, cancer, and heart disease. Yet there's one condition that has reached epidemic proportions in this country that is receiving far too little attention. This malady can strike anyone, at any age, but it hits the elderly with greater frequency and greater devastation. It's the other heart disease that we call loneliness.

There's no Loneliness Fund to finance programs for the forgotten. There's no American Loneliness Society to research and treat this joy killer, but, fortunately, it does not require expert treatment. It responds well to the sincere efforts of nonprofessionals—provided they *care* ... like the twenty-six third-graders in San Antonio, Texas. They took up writing to lonely elderly people as a class project.

The youngsters got the idea after reading a newspaper story about the number of telephone calls policemen receive regularly from people who are simply lonely. You can be sure that the twenty-six third-graders in San Antonio learned much more than good penmanship.

> No soul is desolate as long as there is a human being for whom it can feel trust and reverence.
>
> GEORGE ELIOT

Enlightened By Faith

Nothing in this world is so marvelous as
the transformation that a soul undergoes
when the light of faith descends upon the
light of reason.

W. BERNARD ULLATHORNE

*E*ither life is an illusion, a fantasy trip, a
journey without signposts down a dead-
end street, or life is real, a migration toward an even greater
reality, a procession of purpose.

Just as love between two people can seldom be dictated
or destroyed by pure logic, so, it seems to me, our belief in
the meaning of life is seldom the product of reason only. A
language of the soul—intuition, perhaps—feeds our faith.

Faith takes over at the point where logic ends. It bridges
the gap between what is knowable and what is believable.
When intellect has revealed to us what *is,* faith reveals to us
what *can be.*

This has always been so. It was so when Moses defied

the odds and led his people out of Egyptian slavery. It was so when Joan of Arc followed her voices. It was so when Martin Luther King Jr. marched his people down the highways toward hope. It was so when Mother Teresa picked up babies from the gutter and gave them love. Faith continues, even now, to span the chasm between the actual and the possible.

By faith Abraham, when called to go to a place he would later receive as his inheritance, obeyed and went, even though he did not know where he was going.

HEBREWS 11:8, NIV

All human knowledge, human endeavor, and earthly progress depends on faith that beyond what we know there is a great world of truth and good will still to be discovered. And this is, in reality, faith in God.

JAMES FREEMAN CLARKE

The Christian as Columbus

> Science may prove the insignificance of this globe in the scale of creation, but it cannot prove the insignificance of man.
>
> BENJAMIN DISRAELI

*T*o be a believer is to be a spiritual Columbus. It is to declare confidence that the world is round when all the hard-nosed realists can clearly see that the world is flat. Belief is the ability to see beyond the known world to the world that can be known. It is certainty that reality doesn't end at the horizon.

A valid faith must be built upon a solid foundation of logic, but intellect is only the starting point for faith. When America's space planners decided a generation ago to put men on the moon, they were branded dreamers by many. To be sure, they were. Yet their dreams were extensions of reason, not enemies of reason. Their belief that astronauts could be walking on the moon before 1970 was unprovable. Some of the technologies and materials needed for such a venture had yet to be developed. Nonetheless, their confidence did not defy what was known, it simply went beyond what was known.

So it is with the Christian's faith. No one can prove that the life of the individual continues beyond the grave. Yet is it less logical to presume humans can live again than to acknowledge that they lived in the first place? Life itself is an unfathomable miracle. Even though science has successfully cloned an animal, that achievement has in no way diminished the mystery of life. It simply means that we have unlocked one more secret of *how* life functions. Scientific discoveries add not a particle to our understanding of *why*.

> *Everything science has taught me—and continues to teach me—strengthens my belief in the continuity of our spiritual existence after death.*
>
> WERNHER VON BRAUN

Tell It Like It Is

Always be prepared to give an answer to everyone who asks you to give the reason for the hope that you have. But do this with gentleness and respect.

1 PETER 3:15, NIV

My pastor one Sunday issued this challenge from the pulpit. He said, "How would you communicate the gospel to someone who was deaf, mute, and sightless?" Then he urged us to think of new and creative ways for witnessing. Most of the people around us are, indeed, deaf to our message, unresponsive, mute to it, and blind to its significance. Somehow, we've got to find effective ways of translating the powerful and relevant love of Jesus into positive, contemporary terms.

One way we can do this is to toss out the ecclesiastical vocabulary. The tendency to fall into a certain way of talking is not exclusively a church problem. Every special interest group has its own jargon. Sports fans, soldiers, space technicians, broadcasters—each group has a language that is quite meaningful to members of the in-crowd but virtually unintelligible to outsiders.

Jesus never had this problem, and we modern Christians could take some pointers from his sermons. He always spoke in direct, simple sentences. Parables. Stories. Contemporary and colloquial speech. These were his tools. And Jesus was the most effective communicator the world has ever known.

The people to whom he spoke knew exactly what he was talking about. He didn't try to bowl them over with a lot of technical jargon he'd dug up from ancient scrolls. Jesus told it like it was, and he told it so that his audience got the message.

> *Jesus Christ, in his infinite wisdom, used the words and idioms that were in use among those he addressed. You should do likewise.*
>
> JOSEPH CAFASSO

God to the Rescue?

> What are human beings that you are
>   mindful of them...?
> Yet you have made them a little lower
>   than God,
> and crowned them with glory and honor.
> You have given them dominion over the
>   works of your hands; you have put all
>   things under their feet.
>
> PSALM 8:4-6, NRSV

*F*rom the sad shape of things, it should be evident that operationally, at least, God has put the whole world in man's hands. God has given us the options. Norman Vincent Peale once said, "Order and certainty govern nature. The moon obeys the laws of gravity. The rabbit in the road and the owl are controlled by instinct. But in the life of the human being there is nothing fully predictable, for man—man alone—can alter his environment and change his future. God has given him a will of his own and left it free."

Remember that Adam and Eve, according to the biblical account, had a pretty good thing going in the Garden of Eden. But God had given them the freedom to choose. When they made the wrong choice they were required to pay a severe penalty.

The people of Noah's time brought destruction upon themselves by exercising their options and making bad decisions. Time and time again the ancient Israelites lost their way, spiritually and literally, because they chose unwisely.

There is no basis in the Bible or in history for concluding that whatever we do, however foolishly or selfishly we behave, God will inevitably rush to the rescue.

> Half the world is starving; the other half is on a diet. We are not privileged because we deserve to be. Privilege accepted should mean responsibility accepted.
>
> MADELEINE L'ENGLE

Making God Look Bad

> And God blessed them, and God said to them, "Be fruitful and multiply, and fill the earth and subdue it; and have dominion over the fish of the sea and over the birds of the air and over every living thing that moves upon the earth."
>
> GENESIS 1:28, RSV

Too often we have overemphasized God's role in the world while overlooking our own. We have talked much of God's will. Now, perhaps it's time we talked of our will, for God has put us in charge here. Hatred, war, selfishness, injustice, hunger—these are not God's will. They are the consequences of our willfulness.

Sometimes I think our failures invite the challenge, "Well, if there is a God, and if he's supposed to be kind and loving, how can he permit suffering? How can a good God let little children starve or be killed and orphaned in war?"

The question ignores our obvious role in the continuing creative process. Scripture clearly teaches that we have been given dominion over the earth. We have been charged not only with replenishing it, but also with tending it. God cannot deny us the right to do wrong, because that would reduce us to the level of animals or insects. The same freedom of choice that permits us to be noble and compassionate also allows us to be greedy and hateful.

The question also ignores an obvious law of life that Paul stated this way: "Do not deceive yourselves.... A person will reap exactly what he plants" (Gal 6:7, TEV). We fight, we kill, and we suffer because we continue to plant the seeds of war and misery.

> Owe no one anything, except to love one another; for he who loves his neighbor has fulfilled the law. The commandments, "You shall not commit adultery, You shall not kill, You shall not steal, You shall not covet," and any other commandment, are summed up in this sentence, "You shall love your neighbor as yourself." Love does no wrong to a neighbor; therefore love is the fulfilling of the law.
>
> ROMANS 13:8-10, RSV

When Knowledge Isn't Power

> A handful of good life is better than a
> bushel of learning.
>
> GEORGE HERBERT

*O*nce upon a time we thought education, eventually, would solve our most serious problems. We thought that with sufficient knowledge we would put away war. Instead, we learned how to articulate our hatred, but not how to eliminate it.

Once upon a time, we thought science—technology—would save us. That dream went up many years ago in a mushroom cloud over Hiroshima.

Once upon a time we were told that psychiatry would usher in that long-awaited, better world. However, as British psychiatrist Joshua Bierer puts it, "Psychoanalysis promised more than it could fulfill and people have become disillusioned with it."

We must understand the world about us if we're to deal effectively with it. We also need to know ourselves, and psychiatry can significantly increase the dimension of self-awareness. But we should know by now that the prosperous and peaceful world of our dreams cannot be attained through knowledge alone. The answer, ultimately, lies not in our wisdom, but in our will.

We know that we all possess knowledge.
Knowledge puffs up, but love builds up.
The man who thinks he knows something
does not yet know as he ought to know.

1 CORINTHIANS 8:1-2, NIV

Learning and wisdom without moral purpose are unworthy of their lofty names.

GEORGE N. SCHUSTER

Our Sisters' Keeper

> Then the Lord said to Cain, "Where is Abel your brother?" He said, "I do not know; am I my brother's keeper?"
>
> GENESIS 4:9, RSV

*O*ne of the most tragic by-products of urbanization is the way it insulates and isolates people. The sense of interpersonal responsibility for our fellow man seems to shrink in direct proportion to the growth of our cities.

There was a fresh reminder of this in Detroit, when the grief-stricken mother of a little girl, killed by a hit-and-run driver, pleaded unsuccessfully with her neighbors to identify the man at the wheel. She said several witnesses told her privately that they knew who did it, but they refused to tell the police. Six-year-old Sonyra and her cousin, three-year-old LaRhonda, were run down and killed as they crossed a street toward an ice cream truck. All the witnesses to the tragedy clammed up—they didn't want *to get involved!*

America's moral softness is seen clearly in the apathy and the indifference of many.

The forces of good in the world are immobilized less by their adversaries than by their sleep.

E.M. POTEAT

~

Courage is rightly esteemed the first of human qualities because it is the quality which guarantees all others.

WINSTON S. CHURCHILL

Renewing the City

> While Jesus was having dinner at Matthew's house, many tax collectors and "sinners" came and ate with him.... When the Pharisees saw this, they asked his disciples, "Why does your teacher eat with tax collectors and 'sinners'?" On hearing this, Jesus said, "It is not the healthy who need a doctor, but the sick. But go and learn what this means: 'I desire mercy, not sacrifice.'"
>
> MATTHEW 9:10-13, NIV

Our cities are in desperate need of urban improvement, but they just as desperately need human renewal. These are not separate problems but part of the same condition.

Into these centers of crisis and frustration, the church must carry her unique optimism. She must employ her extraordinary vision to see more than there is in everything. She must engage her creative ability to convert the desirable into the actual.

George MacLeod recognized the relevance of Jesus' teachings to the sick, sad, sprawling metropolis. He urged that the

> cross be raised again at the center of the marketplace as well as on the steeple of the church. I am recovering the claim that Jesus was not crucified in a cathedral between two candles, but on a cross between two thieves; on the town garbage heap; at a crossroad so cosmopolitan that they had to write his title in Hebrew and in Latin and in Greek … at the kind of place where cynics talk smut, and thieves curse, and soldiers gamble. Because that is where he died. And that is what he died about. And that is where churchmen ought to be, and what churchmen ought to be about.*

The Christian view recognizes that cities are both houses and human beings, places and people, environment and inhabitants. When we see the city like it is, and when we see the gospel like it is, we know they were meant for each other.

> *The church and the Christian are not in the world to hate it but to love it with a redemptive love.*
>
> JOHN F. MURPHY

*From the introduction to Carl F. Burke, *God Is for Real* (New York: Association Press, 1966).

Many Happy Returns

All worldly joys go less
To the one joy of doing kindnesses.

GEORGE HERBERT

Simon and his wife, Charlotte, lived in the Detroit suburb of Livonia, Michigan. Traditionally, they celebrated their birthdays together because they were only one day apart. One year they had planned a trip. Then Simon and Charlotte got a better idea: that year, instead of doing something for each other, they decided to do something for somebody else.

So they went to the Starr Commonwealth Home, which cared for two hundred boys, ranging in age from ten to fifteen. Some were from broken homes, some had been referred by juvenile courts throughout Michigan—most were orphans. The couple invited thirty-one youngsters from the home to be their guests at lunch. Then, they took all thirty-one to an afternoon performance of *The Lion King*.

It was a day those boys would remember for a long, long time.

Perhaps Simon and Charlotte finally discovered an ideal gift idea for people to give who have everything.

> Religion that God our Father accepts as pure and faultless is this: to look after orphans and widows in their distress and to keep oneself from being polluted by the world.
>
> JAMES 1:27, NIV

Peace and Conflict

Peace I leave with you; my peace I give to you; not as the world gives do I give to you. Let not your hearts be troubled, neither let them be afraid.

JOHN 14:27, RSV

*T*he church needs the most courage when the conditions of life are least favorable. One writer has described courage as grace under pressure.

Christians need quiet time to think about life, to meditate on Scripture, and to communicate with God. Yet such times of reflection must be a preparation, not an escape. They must be followed by encounter and engagement in the real world of action. Christians are to confront evil and suffering, not as crusaders who consider themselves superior, but as flawed human beings committed to improving life for everybody. Real Christians have, traditionally, moved out of the comfort and tranquillity of the church and into the streets, where people are hurting.

Jesus did proclaim inner peace to individuals, but it was not peace at any price. Babies in the womb are at peace. People who remain intellectually and spiritually unaware also may be at peace, but it is a false peace, enjoyed at the expense of reality.

A real Christian willingly walks into the heat of conflict.

> *I call it an illusion for Christians to seek peace, as though the gospel wanted to make life comfortable for them. As long as the fight is going on, we have peace only in the fight. Our peace is not a well-being; it is a participation in Christ, in God in the flesh against all other things in the flesh.*
>
> CHRISTOPH FRIEDRICH BLUMHARDT

Passion for Adventure

> Religion is full of difficulties, but if we are often puzzled what to think, we need seldom be in doubt what to do.
>
> JOHN LUBBOCK

When the world is a tempest, the Christian should be out battling the waves.

Not moored at the dock.

Not sitting on shore waiting out the storm.

Whatever the challenge is churning up, the person of faith is anxious to take it on.

One clear mark of the believer is a willingness—even an eagerness—to engage reality. To experience existence in all its fullness. To venture with passion into this mystery we call *life*. To confront evil and injustice in all their forms and *contest* them.

Some people mistakenly view Christianity as a refuge for the timid. A place of solace for the scared. But true faith is a sword and a shield—not a bunker. It's having something worth living for, worth working for, and, if necessary, worth dying for.

The real world—the broken and hurting world into which Christians are called—is a world of action. Christians may disagree on beliefs, style, methods, creeds. and sacraments.

But there is little room for debate about the core Christian mandate: Jesus was very clear that the two greatest commandments are to love God and love each other. For him, love wasn't an emotion. It was an event. In his life and in his death, he demonstrated that the quality of love is measured not by what we feel but by what we do.

> *Three times I have been shipwrecked; a night and a day I have been adrift at sea; on frequent journeys, in danger from rivers, danger from robbers, danger from my own people, danger from Gentiles, danger in the city, danger in the wilderness, danger at sea, danger from false brethren; in toil and hardship, through many a sleepless night, in hunger and thirst, often without food, in cold and exposure.*
>
> 2 CORINTHIANS 11:25-27, RSV

Life Purpose

The most intellectually honest person must make some basic assumptions about life. Is it less honest to presume that life has ultimate meaning than to presume it does not? Is it less honest to presume that death is only a phase than to presume it is a finality? Many writers have pondered this question.

In his poem "Johnson Over Jordan," J.B. Priestley writes, "There is in me something that will not rest until it sees Paradise...." Malinowski has perhaps spoken for all of us when he says: "Nothing really matters except the answer to the burning question, 'Am I going to live or shall I vanish like a bubble?' What is the aim and issue of all this strife and suffering?"

If life is no more than a cosmic accident, a mindless joke, a swirl of confusion and color splashed across the black backdrop of meaningless time, then perhaps the techno club is humanity's truest expression of reality. There, bathed in the flashing brilliance of multicolored strobes, rocked by the pulsating rhythms of the electronic beat, stimulated by the sensuous gyrations of dancers—there would be a microcosm of the story and the glory of life.

If, however, life is the considered output of love and intellect; if human existence is the product of purpose; if life is more than something to do while waiting to die; then the truest expression of reality is living purposefully.

> *Our business on earth is to be colonizers of heaven, to redeem the world and set up in it an order of life which will incarnate the spirit and principles of Jesus.*
>
> HALFORD E. LUCCOCK

The Secret of Contentment

> *Life, even the hardest life, is the most beautiful, wonderful, and miraculous treasure in the world.*
>
> PITRIM A. SOROKIN

There's probably no more awesome sight than the night sky when countless stars shimmer against the blackness of space. Yet even this incredible experience can become mundane. After so many nights of looking, we may develop a sort of "been there, done that" attitude.

The heavens are not the only thing, however, that lose their enchanted luster to the dull glow of familiarity:

The job we once thought we'd die for now creaks and groans with the drudgery of routine.

That special person we thought we couldn't live without now greets us each morning with the uninspiring regularity of habit.

So, we jump from job to job and from relationship to relationship, looking for the lost spark that familiarity seems to have extinguished.

Perhaps we're looking in the wrong places. Maybe we need to revisit the places where we already are, to see them again as we did for the first time. A friend once found English writer Gilbert K. Chesterton packing his bags and asked where he was going. Chesterton said he was going to Chamberwell. The friend was astonished.

"Gilbert," he said, "you're already *in* Chamberwell. This is where you live."

"I know," Chesterton replied. "And that's why I'm going away. I'm too close to Chamberwell to see it properly. Things have become too familiar for me to notice them."

> True contentment is a real, even an active, virtue—not only affirmative, but creative. It is the power of getting out of any situation all there is in it.
>
> G.K. CHESTERTON
>
> ∾
>
> I have learned the secret of being content in any and every situation, whether well fed or hungry, whether living in plenty or in want. I can do everything through him who gives me strength.
>
> PHILIPPIANS 4:12-13, NIV

Givers Are Winners

The most prevalent failure of Christian love is the failure to express it.

PAUL E. JOHNSON

*M*odern transportation has shrunk our entire world into a neighborhood. While we don't yet seem willing to make this neighborhood into a brotherhood, it is in our own self-interest to share our abundance with the less fortunate.

Self-interest, of course, is the lowest form of motivation for doing what is morally right. Jesus taught not only service to strangers, but love for enemies. In fact, he emphasized attitude. Undoubtedly, the world would be better if we did what was right; but it would be best of all if we did what was right for the right reasons.

Once I read a New Year's resolution that stated: "I will try at least once each day to offer an unexpected compliment to someone who can't possibly do me any good."

How refreshing to encounter people who do good without an angle. Such people are the winners in the world.

Their trophies include self-respect, sense of purpose, and peace of mind. Even the poorest among us can possess these qualities, but the richest among us cannot buy them.

Byron Frederick says the world is composed of takers and givers. The *takers* eat better. But the *givers* sleep better.

There is encouraging evidence that many Americans, especially young people, are beginning to discover this ancient and inviolable truth: *Keepers are losers.* Or, to state it in the positive: *Givers are winners!*

> *If God allows some people to pile up riches instead of making themselves poor as Jesus did, it is so that they may use what he has entrusted to them as loyal servants to do spiritual and temporal good to others.*
>
> CHARLES DE FOUCAULD

A Learning Experience

To teach is to learn.

JAPANESE PROVERB

*M*rs. Thompson was a fifth-grade teacher. She tried hard to love all her students equally, but Teddy was difficult. He slouched in his seat, didn't get along well with other kids, and turned in sloppy work. Mrs. Thompson began to delight in writing big red Fs on his papers.

Then she began to review his file. Teddy's first-grade teacher had written: "Teddy is a bright child with a ready laugh. Neat work. Good manners."

His second-grade report: "An excellent student, but troubled by his mother's terminal illness. Life at home must be a struggle."

The third-grade report: "His mother's death has been hard on him. He tries, but his father doesn't show much interest."

His fourth-grade report: "Teddy is withdrawn, shows little interest in school, has few friends, and sometimes sleeps in class."

That understanding changed Mrs. Thompson, and she began to value Teddy and treat him with kindness and respect. When Teddy brought her a Christmas gift in a brown grocery bag, other children laughed. When Mrs. Thompson removed a rhinestone bracelet with some stones missing and a perfume bottle only a quarter full, they laughed louder. But they quieted when Mrs. Thompson placed the bracelet on her wrist and dabbed on some of the perfume.

When Teddy grew up, he told everyone that Mrs. Thompson was his all-time favorite teacher.

He invited her to his wedding. She sat in the front row, wearing that rhinestone bracelet and the same brand of perfume Teddy had brought her so many years before. And the teacher dabbed her eyes as she reflected on how much this student had taught her about life.

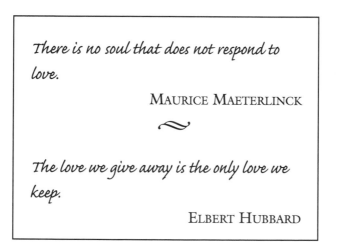

> There is no soul that does not respond to love.
>
> MAURICE MAETERLINCK
>
> ~
>
> The love we give away is the only love we keep.
>
> ELBERT HUBBARD

The Test of Love

> [Jesus asked:] "Which of these three . . . proved neighbor to the man who fell among the robbers?" He said, "The one who showed mercy on him." And Jesus said to him, "Go and do likewise."
>
> LUKE 10:36-37, RSV

A sign in a Greenwich Village shop reads: "I love humanity, it's people I can't stand."

That simple slogan speaks volumes about the love problem today. It is easy to love in general. To love specifically is something else. We may, for instance, believe we love African-Americans as a race, but find it difficult to love the black family that moves in next door.

The true test of love is how a person reacts in specific circumstances. Theoretical love is irrelevant. To be valid, love must come into focus in particular situations. Do you recall that song "The Old Time Religion"? Remember the part that asserts "It makes me love everybody"? That's a worthy sentiment. It has the ring of companionship and togetherness, but is it always true? Sometimes we can sing enthusiastically about love without recognizing our own lack of compassion.

Of course we love our neighbors. However, when we get down to specifics, we are sometimes finicky about whom we are willing to call *neighbor*.

No matter how much the word *love* has been misunderstood or abused, however, it remains at the heart of the Christian faith. Christians are called to be lovers.

> *Christian love is growing interest in, appreciation of, and responsibility for every person as a member of one family of God.*
>
> PAUL E. JOHNSON

The Challenge of the Cross

> *If anyone would come after me, he must deny himself and take up his cross daily and follow me.*
>
> LUKE 9:23, NIV

*T*he challenge of the cross demands total awareness. It insists on touching life, tasting it, grappling with it. It compels us to experience. But Jesus' followers won't settle for illusion or make-believe. They must see life like it is.

To deal with life as it is demands spiritual resilience. Flexibility. For life is not static, but dynamic. Life, as Jesus lived it, was much more than going by the book. He introduced a quality of life that was too big to fit into a rule book. Mercy was more important to him than law; justice was more important than order.

Jesus had a knack for hanging around with the wrong people: the social outcasts, the mentally disturbed, the profane, the swindlers, the prostitutes. He plunged into life with vigor. Like a good physician, he went where sick people were. There were no isolated wards for this great healer. He never ducked danger, and his steadfast, dogged response to the challenges of human need led him to an early death.

Christ's followers today must recognize that apathy is the supreme sin, and compassion the supreme ideal. The failure to care is the gravest injustice we can inflict on fellow human beings—the failure to love, to act in their behalf.

Real Christianity means leaving the comfort and tranquillity of the pew and moving into the world of sweat, blood, and tears.

> *I must be willing to give whatever it takes to do good to others. This requires that I be willing to give until it hurts. Otherwise, there is no true love in me and I bring injustice, not peace, to those around me.*
>
> MOTHER TERESA

No Survivors?

I'd known Freida for more than ten years, so I was a bit shocked to read in her obituary that she left no survivors. Freida was such a warm, friendly, funny, outgoing person. It was hard to imagine her without brothers or sisters, without children or nieces or nephews.

No doubt it was factual to report that Freida had no survivors, but it wasn't true. You see, facts and truth may not be the same thing. It may be a *fact* that Freida left no flesh-and-blood relatives to mourn her passing. But the *truth* is, so very much survived this marvelous lady:

Freida is survived by the dynamic work she launched on behalf of senior citizens. No one was more dedicated, or tireless, in fighting for the rights of our community's elderly.

She is survived by an army of grateful men and women in nursing homes, whose lives are richer because of the watchdog organization Freida founded.

She is survived by the memories her friends cherish of a bright, articulate woman with a bawdy sense of humor who frequently made her point, not with overblown hyperbole, but with an understated quip.

During her seventy-seven years on this earth, the sometimes fiery, always feisty Freida never found time to marry and have children, and her parents died long ago.

But no survivors?

Don't you believe it.

Every last one of us will leave survivors. We can only hope our legacy will be as positive as the one Freida left.

> *There is no higher road than that of charity, and none but the humble walk therein.*
>
> AUGUSTINE

Against the Grain

> Blessed are you when men revile you and
> persecute you and utter all kinds of evil
> against you falsely on my account. Rejoice
> and be glad, for your reward is great in
> heaven.
>
> MATTHEW 5:11-12, RSV

*D*on't expect a medal for taking the high road of Christian commitment. When you make it harder on yourself simply because it's right, you stand out. When you insist on taking life seriously, you seem different. When you go against the grain to embrace a high ideal, a lot of people won't understand. Your refusal to slack off may cause some to question your maturity and judgment.

So let's once and for all abandon the notion that those people who commit themselves to Jesus' way will automatically earn respect. Those who sincerely try to love their enemies may be regarded as gullible. People who sincerely attempt to befriend those who mistreat them may be branded as stupid. Those who insist on turning the other cheek may get slugged. This should not surprise us. It is precisely what Jesus predicted.

Somewhere along the way, we got our theology twisted. We began to think of Christianity as simply another name for respectability. Christians won't always come off looking like the good guys. Sometimes they must oppose their peers, go against the group. They should not be shocked if such behavior makes them unpopular.

The first demand which is made of those who belong to God's church is that they shall be witnesses of Jesus Christ before the world.

DIETRICH BONHOEFFER

Christianity is always out of fashion because it is always sane. And all fashions are mild insanities.

G.K. CHESTERTON

Opposing Oppression

> Render to Caesar the things that are
> Caesar's, and to God the things that are
> God's.
>
> MARK 12:17, RSV

For the most part, Christians are law-abiding citizens. Yet when any law is so obviously unfair or unjust that it inflicts harm upon any segment of society, we should oppose it. We should work to get it changed. We may even be compelled to disobey it and pay the consequences.

Some believe, however, that Christians must obey all laws without question. That view does not follow the teaching and example of Scripture—from the refusal of three young Hebrews to bend before an earthly head of state to Jesus' refusal to answer Herod's questions. The latter was a clear violation of Roman law, and Jesus had no fifth amendment to give legal sanction to his silence. Thousands of Christian martyrs, from Stephen onward, could have saved their lives if they had bowed submissively before the lawful forces of oppression.

Anyone who concludes that the way of the cross is the way of passive submission to all laws should contemplate where such a conclusion leads. It would morally condemn every early Christian who met clandestinely in the catacombs. It would morally exonerate every Nazi who carried out his orders, no matter how brutal or inhuman. It would censure those colonial revolutionaries who defied England to forge out a new, free society. It would excuse those who crucified Jesus under the lawful orders of the Roman regime.

When principle and law come into conflict, principle must take precedence.

> The Proconsul continued insisting and saying, "Swear, and I release you. Curse Christ!" And Polycarp said, "Eighty-six years I have served him, and he has done me no wrong. How then can I blaspheme my King who saved me?"
>
> THE MARTYRDOM OF POLYCARP

Kindness to Remember

> *The best portion of a good man's life is his little, unremembered acts of kindness and love.*
>
> WILLIAM WORDSWORTH

Sometimes you can't even give money away.

It was a publicity stunt on the streets of Las Vegas. The man's job was to pass out dollar bills. Funny thing is, most people wouldn't take them. Some, when they realized what he was doing, crossed the street so they didn't have to get close to this "nut case." They figured there had to be a hook in there somewhere. Maybe we're shocked by unexpected, unexplained acts of goodwill because we're so unaccustomed to them.

An informal movement has developed that encourages spontaneous thoughtfulness. This organization's T-shirt proclaims, "Practice Random Acts of Kindness." Since reading about this group, I've been looking for such random acts—and finding them. For instance, I was told about a young man who stopped to help an older woman change her flat tire and who refused to accept any money for his good deed. I watched a woman as she dropped money into somebody's parking meter.

No name.

No fanfare.

No credit.

Just a random act of kindness toward a fellow human being.

> Lord, make me an instrument of your peace!
> Where there is hatred, let me sow love,
> Where there is injury, pardon.
> Where there is doubt, faith.
> Where there is despair, hope.
> Where there is darkness, light.
> Where there is sadness, joy.
>
> FRANCIS OF ASSISI

Pitfalls of Prosperity

> Not a single outstanding teacher of moral wisdom has failed to warn that riches tend to isolate their owners, make them petty, vulnerable and a little ridiculous.
>
> BERNARD IDDINGS BELL

*T*he pitfalls of prosperity have always challenged Christians, but perhaps never as much as they do today. Affluence tempts us to figure that we have made it on our own. We come to believe that our wealth is a just reward for initiative, ingenuity, and hard work. Well, that may be partly true. But such an attitude lacks both gratitude and humility. It fails to recognize the help others handed us as we climbed the success ladder. It fails to acknowledge those quirks of fate—those happy accidents—that contributed to our prosperity. Above all, such an attitude fails to take into account opportunities and talents that, through no effort on our part, were uniquely ours.

Then there's the temptation to consider wealth God's

gift to those of superior virtue. That view certainly doesn't square with the Bible, nor will it stand up under the scrutiny of our own experiences. The most virtuous man who ever lived was rewarded, not with blue chip stocks, but with a brutal cross. During his final meal with his followers, Jesus predicted that they, too, would suffer if they were true to him.

> *The cross is the only valid symbol for the life of good men. Without it they never see the limits of their goodness. Without it they never understand the arrogance of their self-righteousness.*
>
> J.C. SCHROEDER

A Good Wife

A good wife who can find?
She is far more precious than jewels.
The heart of her husband trusts in her,
and he will have no lack of gain.

PROVERBS 31:10-11, RSV

*I*t wasn't easy for Nathaniel to go home to announce that he had just been fired. He hadn't made much money as a clerk, but it had paid the bills. Now he had to share the shocking news with his wife, Sophia. For reasons he couldn't yet understand, Sophia not only took the news well, she seemed ecstatic.

"Don't you understand?" Nathaniel tried to explain, "I've lost my job. I'm a failure."

Sophia beamed. "You're not a failure. You're now free to write your book."

"We have to eat," he replied somewhat bitterly. "I can't write a book without an income."

Then Sophia opened a drawer and pulled out a hoard of cash.

"Where did you get that?" he gasped.

"Well," Sophia said, "I've always known you were a man of genius. I knew someday you'd write an immortal masterpiece. So every week, out of the money you've given me to run the house, I've saved something. There's enough here to last us one whole year."

Indeed there was. The young clerk who had lost his job spent that year writing *The Scarlet Letter*—one of the finest books ever written in the Western Hemisphere.

Nathaniel Hawthorne went on to become our foremost novelist and one of the greatest literary artists in American history.

It was important that Sophia believed in Nathaniel.

But it was critical that she backed that belief with action.

His achievements, like so many others, came at that intersection where believing and doing meet.

> *I say to you, unless a grain of wheat falls into the earth and dies, it remains alone; but if it dies, it bears much fruit.*
>
> JOHN 12:24, RSV

Good Will Among Men

Christian charity is friendship to all the world—friendship expanded like the face of the sun when it mounts above the eastern hills.

JEREMY TAYLOR

Sharing material wealth is only one form of helping. Giving involves wallets, but it also involves people. No amount of money can staff a hospital with well-trained doctors and nurses unless such skilled people are available. Contributions to seminaries, no matter how substantial, cannot produce ministers unless there are students to attend those seminaries.

Perhaps people have a greater desire to give of themselves than most of us believe. Much of what we label apathy may more often be simply ignorance. To be sure, there are indifferent individuals. Yet what appears to be a lack of caring may be a lack of understanding. In the words of one Roman Catholic priest in Africa: "Everyone wants to help the starving poor. The trouble is, they don't know how."

Millions of Americans sincerely want to do something about the critical problems of our day, but don't know how. They see no clear avenues for direct service. They haven't found handles for their concern.

Many are wondering what they can do in an immediate, personal way to help an abandoned child, a teenager hooked on drugs, or a homeless family. I *sense* more goodwill among us than I *see*. I know that whenever avenues for service open, people respond.

Never be lacking in zeal, but keep your spiritual fervor, serving the Lord. Be joyful in hope, patient in affliction, faithful in prayer. Share with God's people who are in need. Practice hospitality.

ROMANS 12:11-13, NIV

The Heat Is On

> When Jesus prayed for those who had done him to death, we reach the critical point in revelation—that God was in Christ reconciling the world to himself, and that reconciliation must express itself in the reconciliation of man to man.
>
> R. ROBERTS

*H*arry Truman once said that a president who didn't like the heat should get out of the kitchen. The problem is that these days the heat is on all of us and there's no way out. We just have to deal with it. For Christians, the "problem" is also the supreme opportunity. Today the church is challenged to heal, to reconcile, to save people from each other and from the heat of their own selfish desires. The ministry of Christ is moving out of the sanctuary and into the mall; out of the church house and into the coffeehouse; out of the pulpit and into a world in desperate need of Jesus' compassionate message.

One of the biggest tasks facing us is reconciling opposing

views and estranged people. It is perhaps the most difficult challenge of discipleship. We must place ourselves in the middle of conflict and strife, and work for reconciliation.

Jesus said, "Blessed are the peacemakers." He meant, *good for those who get involved in the fight in order to bring about peace.*

Christians are called to be agents of reconciliation. That means exposure to misunderstanding and hate, so that understanding and love might be brought in as their replacements. Christians are people who won't be looking around for the door when the kitchen gets hot. They'll simply loosen their collars, roll up their sleeves, and go to work.

> *Clothe yourselves with compassion, kindness, humility, gentleness and patience. Bear with each other and forgive whatever grievances you may have against one another. Forgive as the Lord forgave you. And over all these virtues put on love, which binds them all together in perfect unity.*
>
> COLOSSIANS 3:12-14, NIV

International Harmony

> What a cruel thing is war: to separate and destroy families and friends; and mar the purest joys and happiness God has granted us in this world: to fill our hearts with hatred instead of love for our neighbors, and to devastate the fair face of this beautiful world.
>
> ROBERT E. LEE

*W*ise men have always admitted the folly of fighting. But somehow foolish people never seem to recognize its ultimate futility. However, violinist Isaac Stern once came up with a novel alternative to war.

Stern suggested that musicians ought to be the world's leaders. If we had maestros instead of politicians in Washington, Belgrade, and Baghdad, the whole world might be marching to more peaceful drums.

Under Stern's plan, when nations had a *score* to settle, they would simply mobilize their woodwind regiments, their stringed divisions, and order them into symphonic combat. For the true militarists, there would always be marching band contests, complete with uniforms and banners unfurled. Nations could carry on their police actions in recital halls around the globe. Their really big, all-out conflicts would be staged in some super battlefield—such as the Astrodome.

Admittedly, it's a crazy approach to solving international disagreements.

Almost as absurd as war.

Since wars begin in the minds of men, it is in the minds of men that the defenses of peace must be constructed.

UNESCO CHARTER

~

They shall beat their swords into plowshares,
and their spears into pruning hooks;
nation shall not lift up sword against nation,
neither shall they learn war any more.

ISAIAH 2:4, RSV

Appeal to Young People

> There is no kind of serviceable labor to increase human happiness and human welfare which may not rightly be called a Christian vocation.
>
> GEORGIA HARKNESS

*I*t is imperative that young people with heads full of idealism and hearts full of commitment dedicate their lives to serving society. As legislators, as journalists, as members of state and defense departments. As teachers, doctors, lawyers, ambassadors, and broadcasters.

Science and industry provide unprecedented challenges to those who would forge a new and better world. The media and the arts today often seem bankrupt of faith and incapable of inspiring hope and confidence. How critical is the need for Christian writers, producers, broadcasters, and actors.

The arts and media are not to be condemned for telling it like it is. But is there no room for creative expressions of how it ought to be? Is there no place on the stage, the screen, the radio, or the television for moral courage, hope, and assurance?

Our world needs young people who will demand a rearranging of priorities. America needs to be goaded and prodded into rethinking and redefining its values. The mass media are too important, too powerful, too influential to be ignored by people of faith.

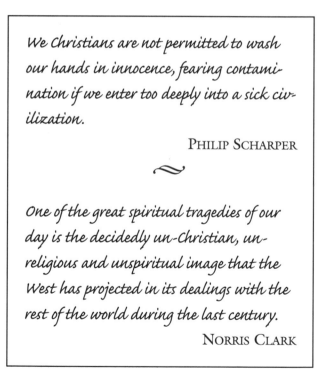

We Christians are not permitted to wash our hands in innocence, fearing contamination if we enter too deeply into a sick civilization.

PHILIP SCHARPER

One of the great spiritual tragedies of our day is the decidedly un-Christian, un-religious and unspiritual image that the West has projected in its dealings with the rest of the world during the last century.

NORRIS CLARK

Little Buckets

A man finds joy in giving an apt reply—
And how good is a timely word!

PROVERBS 15:23, NIV

∾

A word aptly spoken
is like apples of gold in settings of silver.

PROVERBS 25:11, NIV

Words are buckets that carry thoughts. Unfortunately, the way we mishandle them, they sometimes arrive at their destination empty.

This often happens in our conversations with those outside the Christian fellowship. Many people, for example, don't know how to respond to questions such as, "Are you saved?" or "Have you accepted Jesus as your personal Savior?" They are puzzled because the words don't convey meaning to them. They cannot seem to find any content in those particular buckets.

I suggest that we avoid using words like *salvation* or

redemption when telling others about the gift Jesus brought to humankind. Instead, let's speak plainly, as Jesus did. He chose a much simpler word to appeal to his hearers' hearts: *Life.*

No word in itself is good or bad, holy or profane. For example, I learned from my Aunt Vera, a missionary to Kenya, that some words that are perfectly respectable in the United States are used as profanity in Africa. Words themselves are neutral containers. It's the thought the word carries that communicates to others. If we Christians can abandon our attachment to jargon and use plain talk in our conversations, we can recapture the vitality and the crispness of the Good News. As a professional communicator, I believe it's worth a try.

Jesus and his followers spoke in the vernacular of their day. We should follow that example.

> If we continue investing our spiritual energies in words which have become overloaded with the baggage of centuries, it has to be asked if God's word can still speak to us today with power.
>
> MARY GREY

One Hole at a Time

> The present is that part of eternity dividing the domain of disappointment from the realm of hope.
>
> AMBROSE BIERCE

*I*t was supposed to be an easy victory, but it turned out to be an upset. During a postgame interview, the losing coach gave this view of what happened:

"We thought next week would be our tough game. This one was supposed to be a pushover. I think the team was so preoccupied with the *next* game, they forgot to play *this* one."

Pro golfer Tom Kite, a former U.S. Open champion, puts it this way: "You can only play one hole at a time. So focus. Don't worry about the bad shot behind you or the tough one ahead. Just play the hole you're playing."

Now that's great advice in sports, in business, and in life. And it's *practical* advice, because you can't do anything about past mistakes or future challenges.

What you *can* do is concentrate on the immediate task, the opportunity of the moment. Give it your best. You'll be much better prepared for the next one.

Winning at games or at life requires concentration. Don't be defeated by frustration over the past or fear of the future. Focus on the play at hand and the final score will take care of itself.

Who of you by worrying can add a single hour to his life? ... Do not worry about tomorrow, for tomorrow will worry about itself. Each day has enough trouble of its own.

MATTHEW 6:27, 34, NIV

Think only of the present, abandon the future to Providence. The good use of the present assures the future.

JEAN PIERRE DE CAUSSADE

Love's Three Ways

> The hungry, the thirsty, the homeless, the
> sick, the naked, the imprisoned—this is
> our docket. They are our mission.
>
> ERNEST T. CAMPBELL
>
> ∼
>
> Don't just pretend that you love others.
> Really love them.
>
> ROMANS 12:9, NLT

*C*hristians must care for God's little people—
the casualties of life. People who are not big
in power, big in attractiveness, or big in reputation, but who
are big with God. Consider these three ways to show we
care.

First, the way of personal helpfulness. That is, on a person-
to-person basis. As Wordsworth put it, those "little, name-
less, unremembered acts of kindness and love." Remember
that outsiders used to say of the early Christians, "See how
they love one another."

The second way Christians minister to God's little people
can be called organized benevolence. Since many human
needs are repetitive, we have established a network of welfare

agencies and service organizations. For instance, if we find one girl wandering the city streets, we arrange for a family to take her in. But when one hundred girls and boys are sleeping in city doorways, we take them to Covenant House or Love, Inc.

Social justice is the third way that Christians help God's little people. We must dedicate ourselves to changing the social structures that produce the hungry, the thirsty, the naked, the homeless, and the imprisoned. Our love must work not only at the personal level, not only at the intimate group level, but at the social and political levels as well. We must express Christian love not only in small acts of personal kindness, but at the ballot box when a vote is registered for the protection of human rights, for better schools, and for more meaningful and efficient welfare programs.

> How roundly Jesus condemns the deep blasphemy of our slick preoccupation with "problems," when all the time there are no such things as "problems." There are only people, people in need. A preoccupation with problems is one of the occupational diseases of being a Christian in the modern world. A propensity for shutting ourselves off from reality behind a smoke-screen of words is the most insidious of the many sins that so easily beset us.
>
> DONALD REED

Ultimate Survival

> *What better can the Lord do for a man,*
> *than take him home after he has done his*
> *work?*
>
> CHARLES KINGSLEY

Serenity in the face of death—this is the ultimate security. It is available to all, but misunderstood by so many. It is what Jesus had in mind when he told his followers: "Peace I leave with you; my peace I give to you; not as the world gives do I give to you. Let not your hearts be troubled, neither let them be afraid" (Jn 14:27, RSV).

Whatever hope modern technology holds for extending human life beyond the normal range of years, it will never be a final answer to the supreme question. There is a Christian answer, a divine assurance of our share in eternal life. The Christian view is not obsessed with preserving the human body, but rests confidently in the immortality of the human spirit. We find the answer not through debate and speculation, but through commitment. That is how Dag

Hammarskjöld, the late U.N. secretary-general, found it: "At some moment I did answer *Yes* to Someone— Something—and from that hour I was certain that existence is meaningful and that, therefore, my life, in self-surrender, had a goal."

As a world statesman, Hammarskjöld played out a meaningful role on this earthly stage against a backdrop of eternal truths. Hammarskjöld's confidence in ultimate meaning did not lessen his consecration to immediate concerns. Rather, such confidence gave meaning to the present.

> *Throughout history those Christians who have accomplished the most practical benefit in this world are those who have believed most fervently in the next.*
>
> GORDON W. ALLPORT

Formula for Christian Living

Love one another warmly ... and be eager
to show respect for one another. Work hard
and do not be lazy. Serve ... with a heart
full of devotion. ... Share your belongings
with your needy fellow Christians, and open
your homes to strangers. ...

Do not be proud, but accept humble
duties.

Do not think of yourselves as wise.

If someone has done you wrong, do not
repay him with a wrong.

Try to do what everyone considers to be
good.

Do everything possible on your part to
live in peace with everybody.

ROMANS 12:10-18, TEV

With these words Paul wrote what may be the closest we can come to a formula for Christian living. His message is a clear call to action. Verbal piety simply wasn't Paul's thing. His commitment found expression not in the sanctuary, but in the streets. Conformity wasn't his bit, either. For Paul, Christianity meant creative response to the needs of others.

We may find God in a church building, but we may also meet him in the arts or along the assembly line.

We may hear God in a hymn, but we may also sense him in a musical masterpiece or a popular song.

God speaks to us through the Bible, but he also may say something through the newspaper, radio, or television, the voice of a friend, the anguished sob of a young widow, or the tormented cry of a crack addict.

God reveals himself through the life of a believer, but he also may communicate through the profound dialogue of a play or a book. Even a controversial book that seems to mock God may speak volumes about the loneliness and despair of troubled people—people he created; people he loves.

Paul knew, as we must learn, that sometimes the greatest insights come not in burning bushes or atop mystical mountains, but in the commonplace clamor. He knew that if God is *anywhere,* he is *everywhere*—both in the church and in the world.

> *And remember, I am with you always, to the end of the age.*
>
> MATTHEW 28:20, NRSV